Social and Cultural Identity

Social and Cultural Identity

Problems of Persistence and Change

THOMAS K. FITZGERALD, Editor

*Southern Anthropological Society
Proceedings, No. 8*

SOUTHERN ANTHROPOLOGICAL SOCIETY
Distributed by the University of Georgia Press
Athens 30602

SOUTHERN ANTHROPOLOGICAL SOCIETY

Founded 1966

Officers 1973-1974

Charles M. Hudson, President

Harriet J. Kupferer, President Elect

Carole E. Hill, Acting Secretary-Treasurer

E. Pendleton Banks, Councilor

Hester A. Davis, Councilor

Malcolm C. Webb, Councilor

Irma Honigmann, Editor

Joseph B. Aceves, Program Coordinator

Carole E. Hill, Program Coordinator

Contents

Preface

A special ambience of ease and congenial discourse has come to identify the Southern Anthropological Society's regional meetings, and none more so than the meeting held jointly with the American Ethnological Society in 1973. The meeting took place March 8-10 at Wrightsville Beach, N. C., hosted by the University of North Carolina at Greensboro and the University of North Carolina at Chapel Hill. Being affinally related to UNC, I know the year of effort that went into ensuring the effortless sessions that appeared to run of themselves. Credit and thanks for that bit of magic go to Thomas K. Fitzgerald, program chairman, and Harriet J. Kupferer, in charge of local arrangements.

The two key symposium sessions on "Social and Cultural Identity," organized by Thomas K. Fitzgerald, initiated the present *Proceedings*. All the papers herein were read at those sessions.

Irma Honigmann
SAS Editor

Introduction

THOMAS K. FITZGERALD

> Without the binding thread of identity, one could not evaluate the succession of situations.
>
> Nelson R. Foote (1951:20)

JUST a few decades ago, anthropologists considered attempts to conduct research in the area of identity as slightly less than respectable. Today we clearly recognize the social urgency of such an enterprise without, however, always being fully aware of its complexities. Thus for this year's key symposium, we decided to look carefully at the concepts of social and cultural identity, especially as these pertain to problems of persistence and change.

Inasmuch as we have two excellent discussants (a psychologist and an anthropologist) who will evaluate points of individual papers, I have chosen by way of introduction first to comment briefly on the complexity of the identity concept (Soddy 1961) and second, to offer a clarification in the usage of the terms *social* as opposed to *cultural* identity (Soddy 1961).

Erikson (1964) defines identity as a universal psychosocial mechanism for adaptation in face of change. It has little objective reality independent of its sociocultural environment. Even to discuss identity apart from its total institutional and cultural contexts poses difficulties.

Therefore the focus of an individual's identity will vary from one sociocultural context to another. For example in a bicultural setting such as New Zealand (where I did fieldwork in 1968 and 1969), the picture is complicated by the fact that Maoris may participate in separate social and cultural spheres (Fitzgerald 1972). They may, in the language of the interactionists, utilize dissimilar perspectives depending on the particular audience for which they are performing (Rose 1962). Maoris have a diverse number of identity bases. In fact Maoris hold a number of identities concurrently, and these multiple identities may be said to enjoy different values or to have different functions.

Anthropologists have used the term *identity* with a variety of referents in mind, and our symposium papers afford ample evidence of its complexity, the range of identity topics being extremely wide. Some of our participants focus on the concept itself; others use the identity construct more as a way of launching into special areas of interest. Hence, the papers overlap such diverse areas as mental health, drug usage, folklore, ethnicity, complex societies, assimilation, entertainment and Pan-Indianism. The far-reaching applicability of the concept may, in fact, be one of its major strengths.

No two authors, then, use the term in precisely the same fashion. Definitions range from identity as role stance (Robbins: "Identity and the Interpersonal Theory of Disease") to identity as panhumanism (Orso: "Folklore and Identity"). Without reifying the term, we might agree that its components include at least the following dimensions: the biological, the social, the cultural, and the personal or existential. Developing an understanding of these several levels of the identity concept will further enhance its usefulness. Certainly such analytical distinctions can help us to avoid overly simplistic models.

Our symposium focuses on social and cultural identity. As analytical constructs, these two terms direct our attention to several kinds of phenomena within the particular environments to which they apply. An important part of any environment is what the interactionists call the "audience." Therefore, before we can understand identity, we must first consider the audiences to which it is directed. There are at least two sorts of audiences or reference relationships: references involving role identification in concrete group affiliations and references concerned with symbolic identifications alone without implying group participation (Ritchie 1969:120). Identity, then, may be conceptualized in a group sense as well as in an individual sense so that one may conceive of an individual holding several identities at the same time and at different levels of relationship.

Identity is multi-functional and multi-dimensional. Furthermore social worlds differ considerably in the sense of identity felt by their participants. To pursue our New Zealand example: As Maoris often belong to two different cultural segments of New Zealand society, they may identify in varying degrees with both, depending upon the situation. If we assume that people organize and direct their behavior through subjectively defined identifications, we may, in seeking to understand their behavior, distinguish between social and cultural identities.

Social identity has been defined as the general process by which an individual learns certain roles expected of him in specific social situations (Brim 1960:144). Goodenough (1965:2-3), in fact, equates social identities with the rights and duties associated with social positions. Identity in this sense helps to establish what and where a person is in social terms in any given situation. Hence social identities vary to suit the social setting.

It is important, however, to distinguish between identities of individuals in specific interaction situations and identity at a group level vis-à-vis some other group, for cultural identity has relevance only in situations of cultural heterogeneity. This is the setting for identity in New Zealand. Maoris adjust to the national culture in terms of situationally specific identities, or role directives; yet, at the same time, they retain a sense of being Maori in cultural terms. Becker (1960:33) has argued for a principle of commitment to account for the fact that people engage in consistent lines of activity. A sense of cultural identity supplies this unifying principle as people strive toward consistency from one situation to another.

Identity, then, is of two sorts: a more or less fixed identity, involving a fairly exact equation of self with group which is the source of cultural or ethnic identification; and a more relative identity, less rigid and more situationally specific, implying a close resemblance of the individual with his role. The former might be called cultural identity, the latter social identities.

Social and cultural identity are closely related but by no means identical processes. As we have indicated, social identities are situational, the individual shifting his behavior with each adaptation to new situational demands. Social identities, therefore, facilitate identity change; they open the individual to experiences that produce new identities, new social stances. Thus social identities may be said to imply change.

Cultural identity, on the other hand, implies stability. Immediate situational interests are subordinated to more general goals that override the social situation. Cultural identity transcends situational adjustments and in doing so gives common meaning, stability, and predictability to the individual's behavior (Becker 1960). Past identities are reconciled and given uniformity despite their apparent diversity.

With these introductory remarks planted in your imagination, we now turn to the papers. Some of our participants will be talking about social, some about cultural identity; but all of them share a common concern with aspects of culture that directly or indirectly relate to the formation, maintenance, and transformation of identities.

REFERENCES

Becker, Howard S., 1960. Notes on the Concept of Commitment. *American Journal of Sociology* 66:32-40.

Brim, Orville G., Jr., 1960. Personality as Role-Learning. In *Personality Development in Children,* Ira Iscoe and Harold Stevenson, eds. (Austin: University of Texas Press), pp. 127-159.

Erikson, Erik H., 1964. Identity and Uprootedness in Our Times. In *Insight and Responsibility* by Erik Erikson (New York: W. W. Norton), pp. 82-107.

Fitzgerald, Thomas K., 1972. Education and Identity: A Reconstruction of Some Models of Acculturation and Identity. *New Zealand Journal of Education Studies* 7(1):45-58.

Foote, Nelson R., 1951. Identification as the Basis for a Theory of Motivation. *American Sociological Review* 16:14-22.

Goodenough, Ward H., 1965. Rethinking "Status" and "Role": Toward a General Model of the Cultural Organization of Social Relationships. In *The Relevance of Models for Social Anthropology,* Michael Banton, ed., Association of Social Anthropologists of the Commonwealth Monographs, No. 1 (London), pp. 1-24.

Ritchie, James E., 1969. "Comments" to Yehudi A. Cohen, "Social Boundary System." *Current Anthropology* 10:120.

Rose, Arnold M., ed., 1962. *Human Behavior and Social Processes: An Interactionist Approach* (London: Routledge and Kegan Paul).

Soddy, Kenneth, ed., 1961. *Identity, Mental Health and Value Systems* (London: Tavistock Publications).

Identity and
the Interpersonal Theory of Disease

Richard Howard Robbins

THE efficiency of any theoretical framework is measured by the types of questions and issues the theory can generate about a given phenomenon. Taking certain aspects of identity theory, I propose in this paper to examine two related issues concerning traditional or folk theories of disease causation and cure to see how the identity concept can illuminate these issues. Both problems are suggested by the numerous studies which purport to demonstrate correspondence between non-Western ritualistic therapy and Western-style psycho-therapy (Leighton and Leighton 1941; Galdston 1963; Kiev 1964; Kennedy 1967b; Bonilla 1969). If such similarities do indeed exist, we need to explain those factors—be they social, psychological, or cultural—able to produce such similarities in therapy. The second problem involves a reexamination of therapeutic strategies to see whether differences between Western and non-Western therapies are more revealing than the alleged similarities. Can we assume, for example, that differences in social organization between large- and small-scale societies dictate different therapeutic strategies?

The identity concept has been utilized in various ways by anthropologists and other social scientists (Robbins 1973). In this paper the concept refers to identity as a person's social position and to identity processes as those means by which a person's position in the social order is established and maintained vis-à-vis others. This approach originates in the works of Charles Cooley (1956), George Herbert Mead (1934), and more recently, Erving Goffman (1959) and Ward Goodenough (1963), and can best be summed up in the following propositions. First, a person's behavior is a function of his view of himself in relation to his physical, social, and cultural environment. A. Irving Hallowell (1955) has emphasized that a sense of self is one of those traits that emerged in the course of human evolution which make normative behavior possible. The existence of a self concept implies an animal that can and must constantly evaluate its position in regard to its behavioral environment and adjust its behavior accordingly. Second, a person's view of himself is fabricated from information received from others. That is, the person will define his social position from behavioral cues received from others. A corollary to this proposition is that any change in a person's conception of himself requires confirmation from others, while any change in the behavior of others toward him will require the person to reevaluate his own social position. Third, social interaction requires some agreement between actors about their relative position within a social field. A person's social field in this framework includes all those actors who have input into the person's view of himself. Finally, the construct assumes that a person's identity is in a constant state of flux; that is, the behavioral processes by which people align themselves in a social field are an ongoing part of social interaction.

Since this construct puts equal emphasis on how others view the person and on the person's view of himself, it is necessary to speak of identity constituents (Miller 1963; Robbins 1973). There is the person's view of himself—his self-identity—or what he perceives his position to be in regard to others. There is the view that others hold of the person's social position, or his public identity. Finally there is the person's appraisal of what others believe his social position to be, or his social identity.[1] Given the above propositions along with the premise that social interaction depends upon some consensus among actors of their relative social positions, then we must conclude that social interaction depends upon some consonance within a social field of each person's self-, public, and social identity.

This framework has one powerful implication of relevance for this paper. It is that a change in one person's identity will initiate a realignment of the entire social field in which that person is operating. To illustrate, in an interaction of two persons if both initially agree on their positions in the interaction and one of the actors subsequently changes his view of himself, of the other, or of how he thinks the other views him, then the other actor must realign his own self-, social-, or public identity if the interaction is to be based on what Anthony Wallace (1967:78) calls an "identity compact"— "social relationships in which claimed and attributed identities are equivalent." One cannot expect total consonance between self-, social, and public identity. Nevertheless within any social field there is a tendency for behavioral processes to produce such consonance (Burton and Whiting 1965:612).

In this paper I contend that non-Western theories of disease causation are based on the assumption that illness is a consequence of breakdowns or changes in patterns of interpersonal relations and that this interpersonal theory of disease is universal in human societies. The first proposition is not new. A. Irving Hallowell (1963), Robin Horton (1967), and Charles Hudson (1972) have made a similar point, and both Horton and Hudson maintain that the theory has considerable viability as an explanation of disease causation. In relation to the identity construct discussed above, I postulate that when illness is a consequence of social and psychological forces operating on the person, a person's health will be a function of the degree of consonance between his self-, social-, and public identity. This assumption is not as radical as it may first appear. Psychologists and psychiatrists (e.g., Sullivan 1953; Allport 1960; Laing 1962) have, of course, long recognized that mental illness has roots in interpersonal relations. What should be avoided is the arbitrary distinction between physical and mental disease, for not only have we been unable to make a hard and fast dividing line between the two, but imbued with the medical model to interpret physical illness, we have rarely tested for social or psychological factors in what we call physical illness.

Robin Horton (1967) in his work on African belief systems holds that we have misunderstood much about traditional or folk theories of disease because of a failure to translate properly the idiom in which the theory is stated. In other words we have mistaken metaphor for reality. If Horton is correct, then explanations of disease causation such as soul loss, sorcery, breaking of taboos, and spirit intrusion are actually metaphorical statements masking a more fundamental meaning. I suggest that these explanations are all statements of the interpersonal theory of disease.

Several arguments support this contention. When we examine native theories of disease causation in the light of the interpersonal emphasis, the metaphor becomes less obscure. For example beliefs about disease that emphasize soul loss may be interpreted as statements about self-loss (Wallace 1967:63), or loss of definition of self. Rubel in his analysis of *susto* (magical fright or soul loss) in Hispanic America concludes: "The *susto* syndrome will appear as a consequence of an episode in which an individual is unable to meet the expectations of his own society for a social role in which he or she has been socialized" (Rubel 1964:280; see also Madsen 1964).

Beliefs that attribute the cause of illness to sorcery may be interpreted in a similar light since accusations of witchcraft and sorcery are easily seen as statements of interpersonal conflict (see Marwick 1965; Wallace and Fogelson 1965). To say that someone has been made ill as a result of sorcery is the same as saying that he is ill because of a dispute with someone over each other's position in the social field. Among the Lugbara for example witchcraft accusations occur when some person attempts to exert authority others do not feel is legitimate (Middleton 1966). In other words witchcraft accusations arise in situations of attempted realignment of social positions.

Theories that illness results from the breaking of taboos may be interpreted as statements to the effect that the person who is suffering from the illness or is responsible for it has engaged in behavior inappropriate to his or her social position and by doing so has threatened the harmony of the entire social field. Spirit intrusions may be viewed as statements of change of self or loss of self (Bourguignon 1965). It may even be worthwhile to seek whether societies with multiple causes of disease utilize the causes to designate different stages of an illness.

In many societies the interpersonal theory of disease is quite explicit. The Tzoontahal Maya for example not only state that social relations are the prime cause of illness, but go so far as to define someone as a patient solely because he is involved in social conflict, whether or not he evidences physical symptoms (Nash (1971:157).

Diagnostic techniques found in small-scale societies also suggest that they recognize the interpersonal aspects of disease. Turner's work with the Ndembu vividly illustrates this with the Ndembu diviner, who in diagnosing some bodily ills, relates the patient's sickness to ruptures and disturbances in his social field. Turner (1964: 232), states: "Divination . . . becomes a form of social analysis, in the course of which hidden struggles among individuals and factions are brought to light so that they may be dealt with by traditional ritual procedures." Nash's (1971) account of diagnosis in a Mayan community documents this process. Using a technique called "pulsing," the curer places his thumb over the pulse at the wrist, inner elbow, or temple. "The logic is that blood passes from the heart and 'talks' at the pulse points, revealing the condition and needs of the heart. The blood of the curer enters into communication with that of the patient when he holds his own thumb pulse against the patient's pulse. He does not look for the physiological symptoms on which modern medicine bases diagnosis, but for what the blood tells about the patient's relations with people in his social environment and for what the heart needs" (Nash 1971:147).

If traditional theories of disease causation do in fact recognize the interpersonal component of disease, then we can expect therapeutic techniques to be directed toward realigning a patient's field of social relations. The most obvious method is to restore or redefine the patient's identity with regard to others in his social field, while at the same time eliciting from these others testimonials as to the patient's position in the social order. Turner (1964, 1969) gives a number of examples of this technique among the Ndembu. For example, the Ndembu perform a ritual cure they call *Isoma* for a woman who has not been able to conceive or who has had repeated miscarriages. They state that this affliction results when a woman is "tied up" by her matrilineal "shades" or ancestral spirits. The *Isoma* ritual is performed to "unblock" her. To appreciate the logic of such therapy it is necessary to know that Ndembu descent groups are matrilineal, but residence after marriage is virilocal. This creates for a Ndembu woman the dilemma of having to choose between allegiance to her husband in whose village she resides, and to her own village, which is the village of her brothers as well as her children. Children often return to their matrilineal village (the village of their mother's brothers) at a fairly early age, and there is constant pressure for them to do so. The mother then is faced with the decision to follow them but give up the marriage, or stay with her husband and part with her children. The Ndembu state that a woman who has been unable to beget living offspring has forgotten her matrilineal shades or has not paid proper attention to them. Put another way, the Ndembu appear to be saying that the woman's relations with her husband are resulting in the misdefinition of her identity with regard to her own kin group. The *Isoma* ritual is so designed that through symbolic repetition, the patient receives from others in her social field—her family, her husband, and her husband's family—information that confirms or redefines her identity vis-à-vis all others. With this dramatic ceremony her relations to her husband, her family and her husband's family are realigned, with the reordering testified to by all present.

The final point to be made here is that beliefs about the periods when persons are most susceptible to illness support the proposition that folk theories of disease causation represent the interpersonal theory of disease. For example folk beliefs frequently hold that persons undergoing crisis rites are extremely vulnerable to illness. Kennedy (1967a) points out that the Nubian *mushahara* taboos center on the idea that persons involved in rituals of birth, circumcision, marriage, and death are in states of what Kennedy calls "sacred vulnerability," and must observe various taboos lest some illness befall them at this time. The identity-interaction construct makes this belief entirely logical. For if identity change is in fact threatening to health, then such rites do indeed make the person more vulnerable to illness. This interpretation also lends another perspective to rites of passage, for since they serve to announce identity changes and produce from others recognition of the change, they function as health rituals as well as social rituals.

Up to this point, utilizing assumptions generated by certain aspects of the identity concept, this paper has argued that the interpersonal theory of disease is a viable explanation of disease causation and that this theory forms the foundation of all non-Western beliefs about the cause and cure of illness. The second problem to which this paper is directed asks to what extent does social organization influence therapeutic strategies. More importantly, assuming that the interpersonal theory of disease is viable and that ritualistic curing techniques are effective, why does the theory and the therapeutic strategies it generates predominate in some societies and not others?

If we recognize illness to be a consequence of disruption in a person's social field, or lack of consonance between his self-, social, and public identity, then three basic strategies can be followed to reduce the conflict or restore consonance. First one can reorder the patient's social field, bringing everyone's identity into alignment, much the same way the Ndembu restore a barren woman's social field. Second one can change a person's social field. Rather than seek to affirm a desired self-image from persons in the social field in which the conflict arose, one can move the patient to a new social field where there is greater possibility of consonance between identity constituents. Third one can remove the patient from his social field, isolating him for however long it takes for the illness to dissipate or for the threat to others to be removed, possibly attempting during the isolation to refashion his identity. The question now is, is the choice of therapeutic possibilities dictated by the differences in scale between traditional and modern societies? I contend that small-scale societies may utilize only the first and third alternatives, while large-scale societies may utilize only the second and third.

Before we discuss this contention it is necessary to outline some of the differences between large- and small-scale societies that would influence therapeutic strategies.[2] Small-scale societies tend to be more physically isolated from other societies, both geographically and socially. Small-scale societies are characterized by relatively closed social fields, as opposed to the more overlapping social fields found in large-scale societies. For example in a closed social field, if person B is signficant to A's view of himself, A is likely to be equally important to B's definition of himself. In large-scale societies where social fields tend to be more diffuse, B may be important to A's view of himself, but B may not even include A within his social field. In small-scale societies, interpersonal relations form a more interlocking network. Hence a change in one person's identity is likely to affect a greater proportion of members of that society. Thus, for example, interpersonal conflict between two persons in a small-scale society is more likely to involve others than such a dispute in a large-scale society. Finally the intensity of involvement between persons in small-scale societies tends to be concentrated in a narrow range of relations (Wilson and Wilson 1945). Now how do these differences relate to therapeutic possibilities?

As mentioned above the first therapeutic alternative is to effect a reordering of the patient's entire social field. In small-scale societies such therapy is not only possible but necessary. Given the closed social field of the traditional society it is feasible to gather at one time and in one place all those persons who make a difference in the person's view of himself. It is also possible for others at the same time to reorder their own social field or their position in the social order with regard to the patient. If such a treatment involves identity change, then unless others also reorder their identity constituents, the therapy will only produce greater lack of consonance in intᵉrpersonal relations. In addition, because of the concentration of involvement in a narrow range of relations and the interlocking nature of interpersonal relations in small-scale societies, the total reordering of the social field is necessary to avoid permanent schisms in the community. In other words one person's illness, if it does indeed involve identity change, will threaten the entire community. It is doubtful, however, whether such therapy can be initiated in a large-scale society. The geographically diffuse nature of its social fields presents difficulties not found in relatively isolated and immobile small-scale societies. Given the overlapping nature of social fields in large-scale societies, it is impossible to isolate a single social field comprising all affected persons. It is possible, of course, to bring together fragments of social fields, but can one significantly reorder only part of a person's social field? For example this type of therapy is similar to what in our society is called family therapy or organizational therapy. However, if one attempts to adjust a person's view of himself with regard to his fellow workers, then given the assumptions of the identity-interaction construct, it is also necessary simultaneously to adjust his view of himself with regard to his family, friends, etc., who in turn must adjust their view of themselves with regard to the person. Such a process in our society is virtually impossible.

The second type of therapeutic strategy is to change the patient's social field. The isolation and closed nature of small-scale society limits this technique. In our own society it is difficult to say how frequently this is done in formal therapy, although it is common enough as an individual alternative.

Finally there is the isolation strategy involving the withdrawal of the patient from his or her social field. This technique is feasible in both large- and small-scale societies. For example the preliminary phases of many traditional ceremonies, such as rites of passage or affliction, often involve the temporary isolation of some participants from the rest of the group. It is common for young girls undergoing first menses to be isolated from others because she may be dangerous to others at this time. One interpretation suggested by the identity construct sees this practice to have real utility in protecting others. Since the identity change being undergone by the girl requires others to realign their view of themselves, her condition does create a state of danger to the entire social field.

The isolation technique is most common to large-scale societies. Generally such isolation tends to be for longer periods than in small-scale societies and often includes additional therapy. Moreover if the reordering of a person's social field by which the identities of all participants are realigned is indeed impossible in large-scale societies and his transfer to a new social field impractical, then the isolation strategy becomes the logical alternative.

One other particularly interesting point arises about the isolation strategy and the interpersonal theory of disease. It suggests a new relationship between Western medical and psychiatric models of therapy, for both generate therapy that isolates the patient from his social field. In other words the germ theory of disease (as much metaphor as is a belief in soul loss) involves (as does the interpersonal theory of disease) the belief that persons who are ill are threatening to others and must be isolated from the group. One may conclude that the germ theory is another variant of the interpersonal theory of disease, but one particularly suited to societies where the dominant therapeutic strategy must be the isolation of the patient from others.

This paper has been an exercise in drawing implications from a theory. It has raised questions and viewed beliefs about disease and therapy from the perspective of the identity construct. Specifically, it has suggested that there is more unity than generally supposed in non-Western theories of disease causation and that therapeutic strategies are limited by the nature of social organization. In this regard it has implied that non-Western curing techniques may be far better adapted to small-scale societies than modern, Western therapeutic techniques.

Finally this paper may shed light on such practices as couvade (Kupferer 1965), ritual pollution, taboo, and beliefs about death and dying. Since these phenomena in one way or another involve identity change and since identity change involves threats to whole social fields, such beliefs and practices may have real utility in protecting the health of people in a society.

NOTES

1. Various terms have been used by different authors to refer to identity constituents. The terms used here approximate the general usage but are still different from those of some authors. (For a summary of identity terms with their referents see Robbins 1973).

2. This discussion of scale is in part based on the model given by Godfrey and Monica Wilson (1945).

REFERENCES

Allport, Gordon W., 1960. *Personality and Social Encounters* (Boston: Beacon Press).

Bonilla, Eduardo Seda, 1969. Spiritualism, Psychoanalysis, and Psychodrama. *American Anthropologist* 71:493-497.

Bourguignon, Erika, 1965. The Theory of Spirit Possession. In *Context and Meaning in Cultural Anthropology*, Melford Spiro, ed. (New York: The Free Press), pp. 39-60.

Burton, Roger V., and John W. M. Whiting, 1965. The Absent Father and Cross-Sex Identity. In *A Reader in Comparative Religion*, William A. Lessa and Evon Z. Vogt, eds. (New York: Harper and Row), pp. 610-614.

Cooley, Charles H., 1956. *Human Nature and the Social Order* (Glencoe: The Free Press).

Galdston, Iago, ed., 1963. *Man's Image in Health and Medicine* (New York: International University Press).

Goffman, Erving, 1959. *The Presentation of Self in Everyday Life* (Garden City, N. Y.: Doubleday).

Goodenough, Ward H., 1963. *Cooperation in Change* (New York: Russell Sage Foundation).

Hallowell, A. Irving, 1955. *Culture and Experience* (Philadelphia: University of Pennsylvania Press).

―――― 1963. Ojibway World View and Disease. In *Man's Image in Health and Medicine*, Iago Galdston, ed. (New York: International University Press), pp. 258-315.

Horton, Robin, 1967. African Traditional Thought and Western Science I. *Africa* 37:50-71.

Hudson, Charles, 1972. "Sociosomatic" Illness. (Paper read at the annual meeting of the Southern Anthropological Society in Wrightsville Beach, N. C.)

Kennedy, John G., 1967a. Mushahara: A Nubian Concept of Supernatural Danger and the Theory of Taboo. *American Anthropologist* 69:685-702.

―――― 1967b. Nubian Zar Ceremonies as Psychotherapy. *Human Organization* 26:185-194.

Kiev, Ari, ed., 1964. *Magic, Faith, and Healing* (Glencoe: The Free Press).

Kupferer, H. J. K., 1965. Couvade: Ritual or Real Illness. *American Anthropologist* 67:99-102.

Laing, Ronald D., 1962. *The Self and Others* (Chicago: Quadrangle Books).

Leighton, Alexander, and Dorthea Leighton, 1941. Elements of Psychotherapy in Navaho Religion. *Psychiatry* 4:515-523.

Madsen, William, 1964. Value Conflicts and Folk Psychotherapy in South Texas. In *Magic, Faith, and Healing*, Ari Kiev, ed. (Glencoe: The Free Press), pp. 420-440.

Marwick, Max, 1965. *Sorcery in Its Social Setting* (Manchester: Manchester University Press).

Mead, George Herbert, 1934. *Mind, Self, and Society* (Chicago: University of Chicago Press).

Middleton, John, 1966. The Resolution of Conflict among the Lugbara of Uganda. In *Political Anthropology*, Marc Swartz, Victor W. Turner, and Arthur Tuden, eds. (Chicago: Aldine), pp. 141-154.

Miller, Daniel, 1963. The Study of Social Relationships: Situation, Identity, and Social Interaction. In *Psychology: A Study of Science* Vol. 5, Sigmund Koch, ed. (New York: McGraw-Hill), pp. 639-737.

Nash, June, 1971. *In the Eyes of the Ancestors* (New Haven: Yale University Press).

Robbins, Richard Howard, 1973. Identity, Culture, and Behavior. In *The Handbook of Cultural and Social Anthropology*, John J. Honigmann, ed. (Chicago: Rand McNally), pp. 1199-1222.

Rubel, Arthur J., 1964. The Epidemiology of a Folk Illness: *Susto* in Hispanic America. *Ethnology* 3:268-283.

Sullivan, Harry S., 1953. *The Interpersonal Theory of Psychiatry* (New York: W. W. Norton).

Turner, Victor, 1964. An Ndembu Doctor in Practice. In *Magic, Faith, and Healing*, Ari Kiev, ed. (Glencoe: The Free Press), pp. 230-263.

―――― 1969. *The Ritual Process* (Chicago: Aldine).

Wallace, Anthony F. C., 1967. Identity Processes in Personality and in Culture. In *Cognition, Personality, and Clinical Psychology*, Richard Jessor and Seymour Feshback, eds. (San Francisco: Jossey-Bass), pp. 62-89.

Wallace, Anthony F. C., and Raymond Fogelson, 1965. The Identity Struggle. In *Intensive Family Therapy*, Ivan Boszormenyi-Nagy and James Farmo, eds. (New York: Harper and Row), pp. 365-407.

Wilson, Godfrey, and Monica Wilson, 1945. *The Analysis of Social Change* (Cambridge: Cambridge University Press).

Cultural Persona in Drug-Induced Altered States of Consciousness

Marlene Dobkin de Rios

For the anthropologist interested in the use of mind-altering plants in non-Western society, research developments in the last few years have broken ground, stimulating new avenues of investigation to answer basic questions concerning the relationship of the individual to his society and his cultural identity. From a study of the anthropological and ethnobotanical literature on hallucinogenic plants as they have been used in traditional societies throughout the world, there has emerged a greater awareness of the vital role that cultural variables—such as belief systems, attitudes, expectations, and values— have in patterning the visionary experience produced by drug plants. Anthony Wallace's seminal study in 1959 stressed the important role of culture in hallucinatory behavior. Since then, working in natural laboratories where plant hallucinogens are incorporated into cultural activity, or else working backwards in time with archeological materials and art productions of extinct peoples, anthropologists such as myself have attempted to test the hypothesis that cultural variables contribute to the patterning of drug-induced visionary states which are stereotypic in nature (Dobkin de Rios in press a).

The term *stereotypic visions* is illustrated by what I have observed in the Peruvian Amazon among a transitional Indian population— an urbanized, erstwhile peasantry who utilized one plant hallucinogen, ayahuasca (various *Banisteriopsis* species), for the treatment of mental disorders, mainly psychological and emotional in origin (Dobkin de Rios 1972a, b, 1970a, b).[1] Throughout a year's fieldwork I was astounded at the constant recounting by informants of patterned visionary experiences to explain disease etiology. This group held a philosophy of disease causation that set explanations of causality within a matrix of witchcraft or taboo violation. A belief system that focused upon the guardian spirit of the psychedelic vine, ayahuasca, conceptualized a boa constrictor as this spirit. The spirit was believed to enter the circle around which a healer and his patients gathered periodically in the rain forest to treat a disease. Informants repeatedly told of the boa appearing before them while under the effects of ayahuasca. However, despite the negative implications of a large, fearsome creature, this shared vision was believed to be an omen of future healing.

The recent literature on traditional drug-using societies supports Wallace's hypothesis that in a society where mind-altering plants are used in religious or healing activities, cultural beliefs and expectations prepare the individual for a subjective experience that is quite different from the idiosyncratic drug experiences reported in industrial society. In this paper I will explore some areas concerned with how the individual experiences his identity in an altered state of consciousness induced by plant hallucinogens. In particular I will discuss the process of identification whereby the individual accepts as his own the values and interests of a social group. Focusing mainly on Wallace's hypothesis I will look at the way in which cultural membership is experienced at the deepest levels of awareness, accessible through drug-induced experiences. Using the materials on drug-induced states of consciousness I will argue that the most subjective of all experiences available to anthropological inquiry, namely drug-induced ones, point out quite clearly the influence of cultural learning on personal identity. I will explore briefly the data on how stereotypic visionary content is produced in non-Western societies which use mind-altering plants. I will examine cultural persona—the public role or character that a person assumes while under the influence of plant hallucinogens. Although I realize that many of my conclusions are speculative, enough material is available on the importance of plant hallucinogens in traditional societies to justify such an approach.

Recently in delineating a schema of hallucinations that takes cultural variables into account, I had occasion to summarize the literature on the use of psychedelic plants in non-Western society (Dobkin de Rios 1973). Selecting a few societies for which data on drug use is well documented, I will illustrate more fully what I mean by stereotypic visionary content. Then I should like to move into a grayer area to examine how identity in traditional society is experienced during a drug-induced state.

Wallace's (1959) early study of the cultural patterning of hallucinatory experience pointed out major differences in mood, affect, and expectation between a group of native American Indians who ingested peyote (*Lophophora williamsii*) and individual white American drug users. In a monograph prepared for the National Commission on Marihuana and Drug Abuse, I summarized the literature on a dozen societies of the world where plant hallucinogens played an important role in religion and healing (Dobkin de Rios 1973). Some of the better documented cases offer interesting confirmation of Wallace's hypothesis.

The Huichol Indians of North Central Mexico are among the earliest drug users in the new world. Today maize farmers and cattle ranchers, the Huichol were once deer hunters, an activity that is still of great importance to them. Every year they pilgrimage to their aboriginal home in San Luis Potosí, which they claim is their sacred homeland. During a forty-day march full of ritual restraints and personal sacrifice, the Huichol believe they are retracing the path of their ancient mythological heroes who were driven out of their homeland. There is a large, important literature on the Huichol use of peyote during this pilgrimage and subsequent periods (Benzi 1972; Furst 1972; Lumholtz 1900; Zingg 1938). Despite limitations of space we should stress the way in which the religion, value systems, and world view of the Huichol are intricately linked to peyote. Meyerhoff (1970) has pointed out the tripartite symbolic complex which links peyote to the deer and to maize. Huichol ceremonial life consists of obtaining and using each of these three elements in sequence. We can only understand Huichol drug-induced visions within the holistic context of their religion. A French anthropologist, Benzi (1972), has amply documented stereotypic peyote visions interpreted as manifestations of supernatural forces. He points out that when Westerners take peyote, they describe its effects as clearly distinctive from normal waking reality, as experience which is essentially idiosyncratic and individual. The Huichol, on the other hand, have visions which, in Benzi's words, are rarely dissociated from the context of their culture. As with other non-Western societies, the Huichol use peyote as a vehicle to establish contact with their gods. Generally they see manifestations of their gods in the forms of animals such as snakes or jaguars. Often the apparition of a divine animal is preceded by a violent wind, making known the appearance of a sacred creature.

A second important visionary pattern is stereotyped. Very tiny crystals of rocks appear in human form, which Benzi likens to Lilliputians. Shamanistic chants evoke uniform Huichol visions and the shamans themselves have patterned visions which enable them to return to the divine abode, the place of the origin of the gods, where they find the last privileges that man gave up when he transgressed divine laws. Another important stereotypic vision concerns hearing the voice of the first shaman, which is an entrée into the shamanic career. Only those shamans who have attained the degree of required purity see their mythical hero.

Other cultures which report stereotypic visions include the Kofan, studied by Scott Robinson (1972). A montaña people of the Ecuadorian Amazon, the Kofan use ayahuasca, which they call *yagé*, and report visions of plants and birds of nature. In their imagination the Kofan visit herds of wild game to insure their successful hunt in subsequent days. Like other drug-using peoples, the Kofan personify the spirit of the plant. They call the spirits the *yagé* people. Robinson reports that shamans see knowledge revealed to them in four stages. The first level is comprised of geometric figures. After about an hour they become transformed into distinct forms such as wild birds and animals. Continuing to take *yagé*, the shaman begins to suffer from attacks by snakes, tigers, and boas until he feels that he has died. Although people fear the imminence of death, they believe that the shaman's soul separates from the body and ascends to the place where the *yagé* people live. A veritable paradise, there is an abundance of food and drink, and the shaman is taught special chants by the *yagé* people.

Among the Shagana-Tsonga of the North Transvaal a plant hallucinogen, *Datura fastuosa*, is used to achieve religious visions in a female initiation ceremony at puberty. A student of mine, Thomas Johnston (1972), describes the puberty rite in which the *Datura* is given to young women so that they may enter into communication with the ancestor god who grants fertility. He presents evidence that the drug's effects, the synesthesia of music and color, and the effects of the dancing combine to further the goal of the rite, which is to ensure fertility by supernatural means. Johnston points out how the use of the plant hallucinogen is culturally patterned to produce stereotypic visions in which girls hear ancestral voices, especially that of the ancestor god, assuring the initiate of fertility.

Among the Fang of the Northwest Equatorial Africa a powerful mind-altering plant, *Tabernanthe iboga*, has been used in a revitalization cult called *Bwiti* (Balandier 1963; Fernandez 1965, 1972; Pope 1969). Young men at puberty are given large doses of the plant to induce fantastic visions which include seeing the *Bwiti* spirit. The culture hero, *Bwiti*, is an intercessor between man and the gods. His revelation is a means of communicating with an assembly of dead ones, a chain of valued ancestors. The actual *Bwiti* vision is quite elaborate: a macabre form or fantasma arrives to take the initiate by the hand and conduct him across a thousand turns and detours where the initiate sees a long procession of skeletons and cadavers pass in front of his eyes, pale, gesticulating, and giving off an insupportable odor. Fernandez (1972), studying the cult, reported stereotypic visions for the Fang. In a sample of fifty people, forty percent reported seeing dead relatives who instructed them to eat of the *iboga*. An important stereotypic vision shows the initiate walking over a long, multicolored road or over many rivers leading to the abode of his ancestors, who then take the initiate to the great gods. Fernandez stresses how important a Fang's genealogy is for reaffirming his relationship to his ancestors. Therefore, Fernandez (1972:253) argues, the *iboga* visions follow a legendary genealogical framework.

We turn now to questions most pertinent to this symposium: how does the individual experience his cultural or personal identity in a drug-induced state of consciousness?

I should like to make clear at the onset that the psychedelic experience is a complex one that only a concatenation theory of hallucinations can attempt to explain. Thus only a theory incorporating the interaction of antecedent variables—including biological, psychological, social, and cultural—with the consequent use of the drug can predict drug effects. Although an attempt has been made to look in greater detail at these complex interactions (Dobkin de Rios in press b), it is important to reiterate that cultural factors such as enculturation in a shared symbolic system, shared expectation of visionary content, the cultural use of nonverbal aspects such as music and odors (cf. Katz and Dobkin de Rios 1971), the presence of a common belief system and certain values concerning the role of the drug are as important to a theory of hallucinations as any other set of variables. Further complications arise from the variables added by somatic and psychological effects of the drug itself. These effects have been summarized by Ludwig (1969) and include such features as synesthesia (sensory scrambling of modalities) and depersonalization. Recognizing the complex interweaving of a host of variables in a given psychedelic experience, nonetheless, I think we can address ourselves to the problem of how the drug user in traditional society experiences his identity. Whether it is seeing the *Bwiti* spirit, knowing the fertility god among the Shagana-Tsonga, or controlling one's allies and sending them to do one's bidding as among ayahuasca-using shamans, or seeing the Huichol's first shaman, we do find reports confirming the importance of culturally stereotypic visions despite the heterogeneity of personality types in a given culture.

My own empirical data on ayahuasca use in the Peruvian Amazon makes it apparent that it is important to consider the role of socialization in this context. Esoteric beliefs concerning ayahuasca, the expectations of adults as to the effects of the drug, as well as witchcraft beliefs and their philosophy of disease causation are as much a part of daily life as discussions on how to prepare a fish stew or weave a fishing net. Children are never sent away when such topics are discussed. My first contact, in fact, with an ayahuasca healer was through the introduction of an adolescent boy who had formed a friendship with him. From earliest childhood on, boys and girls in the urban slum where I worked learn about the plant hallucinogen. Their learning is perhaps not as direct as in traditional societies. Nonetheless, by being present in family and neighborhood discussions, they acquire many expectations concerning ayahuasca use. The healers are greatly admired and sometimes feared—an emotional reception not lost upon a young child. Throughout the socialization period, in their children's presence, adults openly discuss the revelatory nature of the drug plants since ayahuasca is used to reveal the individual or agent responsible for bewitching and making a person ill. Former patients analyze their experiences of visionary states in retrospect and often recount the brief aspect of their vision that indicated to them or their healer exactly what force was responsible for their bewitchment and subsequent disease. The often-viewed boa constrictor is discussed freely as an omen of healing. Special diets and regimens prescribed by healers are discussed years after a person's illness has been treated. The plant hallucinogen is highly valued and seen to be essentially good, a vine that will aid in the healing process. Ayahuasqueros are said to be knowledgeable about diagnosing and curing disease. The great hardships they incurred during their apprenticeship when they lived in virgin forest areas with little food or salt, earn the admiration of their urban and rural clients. Healers repeat stories of how they took the drug themselves and learned from teachers said to be wise about healing plants.

The urban poor among whom I worked valued such a powerful anti-dote to the evil of people that they believed to be omnipresent.

Assuming the ayahuasca material is generalizable, then in societies where hallucinogenic plants play a central role in structuring belief systems and reaffirming cultural values, their influence on the in-dividual's unconscious is thoroughgoing. My initial response as a Westerner to reports of similar drug experiences was amazement. In reports of Western drug experiences, we find overwhelming evidence for their idiosyncratic nature (Wallace 1959; Ebin 1961; Aaronson and Osmond 1970). In industrial societies like our own, a search for personal fulfillment or for oceanic or transcendent experi-ences may characterize the counterculture's use of mind-altering plants. This does not hold true for the Peruvian data. In contrast ayahuasca is used in a patterned way to make conscious areas of sociocultural stress—mainly figures in the individual's milieu—that can be faulted for illness due to witchcraft. If more data on other drug-using societies were available, we might be able to generalize that stereotypic visions serve to make accessible to conscious experience areas of conflict, strain, practical knowledge, or religious ecstasy when that is valued by a society. We have some evidence from Cordova-Rios's work on how traditional drug-using societies often programmed their drug users to learn about the animals they hunted from the psychedelic experience (Cordova-Rios 1972; Dobkin de Rios 1972c). In much the same way, accepting as one's own the values and interests of a social group can be greatly expedited by the use of plant hallucinogens in traditional society. Some of the examples chosen here illustrate the use of plant hallucinogens during puberty rites when social learning becomes crucial for maintaining social solidarity among diverse groups of people.

To summarize briefly, I am saying that cultural identity is learned and reaffirmed by psychic productions under drug experiences in many traditional societies of the world. The evidence at hand indi-cates that substrata of the personality are indeed highly susceptible to social learning. I would also argue against any attempt to wrench the individual's psyche from its complex interrelationship with the cultural matrix.

Certainly anthropologists interested in the relationship between the individual and his society have much to learn from the analysis of materials on mind-altering plants and the production of stereotypic visions ensuing from their use. These studies, in my opinion, amply show that at deep layers of the unconscious, personal identity has

strong cultural components, most probably resulting from the socialization process.

NOTE

1. The study of folk psychotherapy with ayahuasca was funded by the
Foundations Fund for Research in Psychiatry, G67-395 from June 1968 to
May 1969. A deep debt of gratitude is acknowledged to Dr. Carlos Alberto
Seguin, Director of the Peruvian Institute for Socio-Psychiatric Studies, Lima
for his guidance throughout.

REFERENCES

Aaronson, Bernard, and Humphrey Osmond, 1970. *Psychedelics: The Uses
    and Implications of Hallucinogenic Drugs* (Garden City, N. Y.: Doubleday)
Balandier, Georges, 1963. *Sociologie Actuelle de l'Afrique Noire* (Paris: Presses
    Universitaires de France).
Benzi, Marino, 1972. *Les Derniers Adorateurs du Peyotl* (Paris: Gallimard).
Cordova-Rios, Manuel, 1972. *Wizard of the Upper Amazon* (New York:
    Atheneum).
Dobkin de Rios, Marlene, 1970a. A Note on the Use of Ayahuasca among
    Mestizo Populations in the Peruvian Amazon. *American Anthropologist*
    72:1419-1422.
_____ 1970b. *Banisteriopsis* Used in Witchcraft and Folk Healing in Iquitos,
    Peru. *Economic Botany* 24:296-300.
_____ 1972a. *Visionary Vine: Psychedelic Healing in the Peruvian Amazon*
    (San Francisco: Chandler).
_____ 1972b. The Use of Hallucinatory Substances in Peruvian Amazon Folk
    Healing. (Ph.D. Diss., Department of Anthropology, University of California,
    Riverside).
_____ 1972c. Review of Manuel Cordova-Rios, *The Wizard of the Upper
    Amazon* (New York: Atheneum). *American Anthropologist* 74:1423-1424.
_____ 1973. The Non-Western Use of Hallucinatory Agents. In *Second
    Report of the National Commission on Marihuana and Drug Abuse* (Wash-
    ington, D. C.: U. S. Government Printing Office), vol. 4, pp. 1171-1209.
_____ in press a. The Influence of Psychotropic Flora and Fauna on Maya
    Religion. *Current Anthropology.*
_____ in press b. Man, Culture and Hallucinogens: An Overview. In *Cross-
    Cultural Perspectives on Cannabis* (The Hague: Mouton).
Ebin, David, 1961. *The Drug Experience* (New York: Grove Press).
Fernandez, James W., 1965. Symbolic Consensus in a Fang Reformative Cult.
    American Anthropologist 67:902-929.
_____ 1972. *Tabernanthe iboga:* Narcotic Ecstasis and the Work of the Ances-
    tors. In *Flesh of the Gods: The Ritual Use of Hallucinogens*, Peter T. Furst,
    ed. (New York: Praeger) pp. 237-260.
Furst, Peter T., ed., 1972. *Flesh of the Gods: The Ritual Use of Hallucinogens*
    (New York: Praeger).
Johnston, Thomas F., 1972. *Datura fastuosa:* Its Use in Tsonga Girls' Initiation.
    Economic Botany 26:340-351.
Katz, Fred, and Marlene Dobkin de Rios, 1971. Hallucinogenic Music: An
    Analysis of the Role of Whistling in Peruvian Ayahuasca Healing Sessions.
    Journal of American Folklore 84:320-327.
Ludwig, Arnold, 1969. Altered States of Consciousness. In *Altered States of*

Consciousness, Charles Tart, ed. (New York: John Wiley and Sons) pp. 9-22.

Lumholtz, Carl, 1900. *Symbolism of the Huichol Indians,* American Museum of Natural History, Memoirs, I (New York).

Meyerhoff, Barbara, 1970. The Deer-Maize-Peyote Symbol Complex among the Huichol Indians of Mexico. *Anthropological Quarterly* 43:64-78.

Pope, Harrison, 1969. *Tabernanthe iboga:* An African Narcotic Plant of Social Importance. *Economic Botany* 23:173-184.

Robinson, Scott, 1972. Shamanismo entre los Kofan. In *Proceedings, 39th International Congress of Americanists,* Vol. 4, *Historia, Ethnohistoria y Ethnologia de la Selva Sudamericana* (Lima), pp. 89-94.

Wallace, Anthony F. C., 1959. Cultural Determinants of Response to Hallucinatory Experience. *AMA Archives of General Psychiatry* 1:58-69.

Zingg, Robert, 1938. *The Huichols: Primitive Artists,* University of Denver Contributions to Ethnography I (New York).

Folklore and Identity

Ethelyn G. Orso

In a recent essay Eugene Hammel (1972) discusses a basic anthropological dilemma.[1] He feels that anthropologists have been inconsistent in sometimes arguing that people are all the same and therefore equal, and other times arguing that people are all different and have the right to be so. It may seem paradoxical to claim that mankind is all the same (or shares certain basic features), and that (different groups of) mankind are different; but, there is no necessary contradiction involved. Hammel's observation of the fluctuation in emphasis of these two views in anthropology, rather than their equal emphasis, is germane to this paper.

Although Kroeber and Kluckhohn (1963) have compiled dozens of definitions of the term *culture*, the term has been used in two distinct ways by anthropologists in America. Many American anthropologists trace the origin of the discipline to Sir Edward Tylor, whose definition of culture as "that complex whole which includes knowledge, belief, art . . . and any other capabilities and habits acquired by man as a member of society" (Tylor 1958:1) was generally used by him in the universal sense to imply the basic adaptation of mankind as a whole. A narrower meaning of culture gained emphasis following the impact of Franz Boas in America. Boas, who was skeptical of the discovery of universal laws of behavior, preferred to focus on the particular culture (the Eskimo, the Kwakiutl, the Tlingit) and encouraged his students to make haste to the field to describe and record the culture of peoples who were on the verge of extinction or absorption by Western civilization. Through Boas the term *culture* became synonymous with tribal ethnicity and became identified as the distinct possession of a particular group of people.

Cultural identity in the broader sense is the awareness that universals of culture exist, that people throughout the world face the same life crises and are capable of sharing many attitudes, sentiments, and elements of behavior. Such panhuman cultural identity could become an aid to peace and harmony between groups and nations. If anthropology and folklore have a mission for mankind, it is to promote awareness of panhuman identity.

In the narrower sense, cultural identity is a kind of ethnocentrism. Anthropologists are well aware that ethnocentrism has a positive function to fulfill in maintaining social solidarity and group survival. But ethnocentrism can become a real hindrance to peaceful coexistence when powerful groups act on their beliefs of superiority. To over-emphasize narrow cultural identity is to work against cross-cultural communication. Cultural identity in this sense I will refer to as *ethnic identity*.

Since at least the seventeenth century, scholars and intellectuals have used folklore consciously to promote ethnic identity (Wilson 1972). Folklore has often been a part of a group's revitalization attempt in the face of acculturation pressure by another group (Wallace 1956). At times, (best illustrated by Nazi Germany) the ethnocentrism thus generated became so intense that the group began to force its culture on other groups.

The promotion of panhuman identity began later, in the mid-eighteenth century (Tylor 1964). Ironically folklore has also been the primary implement for those who saw beyond the narrow limits of ethnicity.

It is also possible to distinguish in folklore scholarship the two levels of discourse—the universal and the distinctive. According to Richard Dorson, a leading American folklorist:

> One paradox of folklore studies is seen in their shuttling back and forth between opposite poles of emphasis. The materials of folklore lend themselves equally to comparative, international, or cross-cultural theorizing and to inward, national self-appraisal. The comparative approach stresses the unities and common themes of folklore in many lands, and the nationalistic approach concentrates on the distinctive qualities of the folk traditions found within one country. Where the national folklorist sees in a proverb of common coin the indelible stamp of his people's wit and sentiment, the comparative folklorist dryly points out that the same saying is found in a dozen languages. A neutral observer will remark that a Märchen travels around the world with its narrative core intact, but that the style and mood and descriptive detail vary greatly in its presentation. Accordingly, the theories of the comparative and the nationally oriented folklore scholars can be complementary rather than conflicting. (1963:96)

Although Dorson sees these two trends as possibly complementary, today very few American folklorists even make the effort to give them equal emphasis. American folklorists are not even dedicated to the promotion of a national school of American folklore. Instead most are absorbed in the narrow collection, classification, and analysis of folklore as the unique possession of a particular group. Indeed many specialize (as do many anthropologists) in a particular group. For example Roger Abrahams deals mainly with black folklore and Américo Paredes specializes in Chicano folklore.

Some American folklorists have begun to broaden their focus with applied folklore projects in such areas as desegregation, medicine, and craft revivals. A broader folklore approach would emphasize that different groups of Americans have similar jokes, proverbs, sentiments, and values.

The rest of the paper will trace historically the development of the use of folklore to further these two distinct and sometimes opposing goals. I shall distinguish between the universal folklorists, who accept the psychic unity of mankind and whose work has contributed to the development of panhuman identity, and ethnic folklorists, who prefer to emphasize the differences between groups of people.

The Ethnic Folklorists. William Wilson (1972), in his paper "Folklore and Nationalism in Finland," argues that folklore studies began during the Reformation in the early seventeenth century in Finland in opposition to the Swedification of the country. In 1636 an Antiquities Society was formed to substantiate claims of the antiquity of Finnish culture and language. By collecting songs and poems these early Finnish folklorists argued that they were the sons of Noah and that Finland had been a mighty nation in the past that dominated even Russia. They even argued that Finland had been Atlantis. These seventeenth-century scholars were not zealous nationalists, but the rise of Finnish nationalism in the next century can be traced in part to their early efforts.

In an earlier paper, Wilson argues that European folklorists differed substantially from English and American folklore researchers who have devoted "much of their time to the study of survivals. . . . On the continent serious folklore studies began earlier and followed a different path. They were from the beginning intimately associated with emergent romantic nationalistic movements in which zealous scholar-patriots searched the folklore record of the past not just to see how people had lived in bygone days . . . but primarily to discover historical models on which to reshape the present and build the future" (Wilson 1967:1).[2]

Wilson attributes the rise of European folklore research and nationalism to the writings of the eighteenth-century scholar Johann Gottfried Herder. Herder lived at a time when German culture was dominated by French and foreign influences, a time when Germany was a "masterpiece of partition, entanglement, and confusion. The country was divided into 1800 different territories with an equal number of rulers. There was no unity in commerce and industry, and the air was rife with religious feuds. All this spelled disaster to Herder. He insisted that Germany return to her own foundations or be doomed" (Wilson 1967:8-9). Herder pleaded with his countrymen to cherish their own ways of life inherited from their fathers and to build upon them.

According to Wilson, Herder believed that folk poetry was the highest expression of the national character since it had been preserved by the German peasants who had remained the most unspoiled by foreign influence and who had kept alive the songs sung by German forefathers. In 1773 Herder made one of his first pleas to collect folklore. Among the many who responded to Herder's call were the Grimm brothers whose 1815 collection of folktales have continued in popularity to the present (Wilson 1967:14-15).

Historians credit Herder with the inspiration for creating a united Germany, and his theory of nationalism diffused to many lands (Wilson 1967:18). In Finland, due to Russian domination of Finnish culture and language after 1809, a small group of patriotic intellectuals eagerly followed Herder's philosophy and looked to the past (through Finnish folklore) to find strength for the future (Wilson 1967:19).

Thus modern ethnic folklore research in both Finland and Germany were influenced by Herder. Yet the results of the influence were completely different. In Finland the Finnish Literary Society was founded in 1831.[3] In 1835 the science of folklore research began with the publication of the *Kalevala*, a collection of folk runes and charms compiled by a country physician, Elias Lönnrot. Ever since, the *Kalevala* has remained the major subject of study by Finnish folklorists and of literary reverence by the Finnish nation (Dorson 1963:96). But by the end of the nineteenth century the leading Finnish folklorist, Julius Krohn, recognized that the *Kalevala* was not as ancient as had been believed and also that perhaps the major part of the material had been borrowed from myths and legends of other peoples. However, in a truly scientific spirit, Krohn (1971:14-15) presented his findings to his countrymen. For the Finnish people the reaction was bitter dismay and Krohn's work was no longer accepted with complete enthusiasm. But more significantly,

Krohn's (1971:16) unfortunate discovery led him to create the famous Finnish historical-geographical methods of comparative folklore research. This method is only seldom used in American folklore today probably because of the great amounts of time and effort it requires. However, in Europe it remained until recently a dominant method of the universal folklorists.

Although the Finns began as ethnic folklorists and continue to pursue studies of Finnish culture, today they remain perhaps the world leaders in universal folklore research. Indeed the Finnish folklorists seem to be the most successful in giving equal emphasis to the ethnic and the universal approaches.

In Germany the foundation of modern folklore scholarship can be traced to Jacob Grimm in the early years of the nineteenth century. The emphasis that he gave to the discipline is still characteristic of folklore activities in Germany (Taylor 1961:295). But by the midtwentieth century German folklore scholarship had developed what Dorson (1963:96) calls "evil theory." Germany was

> the first national state to make political capital of folklore studies . . . [under] the National Socialist government of Hitler. During the 1930's, a massive literature of folklore was published in Germany, documenting the Nazi concept of a *Herrenvolk* united by mystical bonds of blood and tongue, culture and tradition. The term *Volk* had ever since the days of Herder possessed a mystical aura, and it now became endowed with political meaning: the *Volk* was the nation. . . . Searching for a spiritual ancestor, the Nazi folklorists . . . [chose] Riehl, a sociologist and travel-writer who in 1858 had written *Die Volkskunde als Wissenschaft*, "Folklore as a Science." The Nazis appreciated Riehl's recommendation that folklore should concentrate on things German and apply this knowledge to practical use. Thus police science could benefit from a knowledge of popular customs and usages. . . . In the late 1920's folklore became a popular subject in some universities, often being an obligatory course. (Dorson 1963:97)

Thus in German ethnic folklore research, the worst of our nightmares came true. Germans became so conscious of their own ethnicity, so ethnocentric through the propaganda of applied folklore, that they turned against and eliminated millions of Jews, Gypsies, and others who were not *Herrenvolk* and thus not human beings.

Today German folklore research remains primarily ethnic in focus, and the bulk of German scholarship involves the collecting of parallels and annotations and the writing of handbooks dealing primarily with German folklore (Taylor 1961:297).

Although the American Folklore Society was founded in 1888, folklore research in America was dominated by anthropologists such as Franz Boas and his students until 1925. Under the Boasian historical particularist approach, folklore studies maintained an ethnic focus. By the 1960s several universities began offering graduate degrees in folklore and the American Folklore Society transformed considerably from an organization dependent on amateurs or academics studying folklore as a secondary interest to an active society primarily supported by trained folklorists (Dorson 1972:5).

Two decades ago, American folklorists under the influence of Stith Thompson at Indiana University showed a strong interest in comparativist activity. Although the interest has not completely ended, today most folklorists understand their discipline primarily as the study of special groups such as ethnic groups, age groups, regional groups, or occupational groups (Bauman 1972:31). In a recent article Richard Bauman (1972) points out that the two most widely used general folklore textbooks, authored by Alan Dundes (1965) and Jan Brunvand (1968), both emphasize folklore as the possession of folk groups. Bauman laments this situation, which he considers a conceptual distortion. He insists that folklore must not be viewed narrowly as a group's possession and identity, but broadly as a group's performance for other groups. He feels that the interaction between two (or more) groups in folklore performance is the key factor that has been omitted from conceptual formulations of folklorists. Bauman is part of the group of American folklorists who wish to break with the older conception of folklore as traditional material and instead consider it a kind of social behavior or artistic vocal performance that is subject to the same kind of implicit and explicit cultural rules that govern all human behavior (Bauman 1972:35-40). Today the American Folklore Society is involved "in something of a clash of interests between the behavioral folklorists such as Bauman and others associated with him at the University of Texas, as well as certain folklorists at the University of Pennsylvania and UCLA, and the nonbehavioral folklorists such as Dorson, Brunvand, and the folklore faculty at Indiana University" (Frank deCaro: personal communication). If the behavioralists become dominant in American folklore, this could lead to a de-emphasis of the ethnic approach and perhaps a renewed association between folklorists and cultural anthropologists.

Up to this point I have been discussing the conscious scholarly use of folklore to promote ethnic identity. However, living folklore is often used by a group of people as a means of distinguishing itself from different adjacent ethnic groups. Although such use may also be conscious, the folklore is not manipulated in the manner of Herder, Lönnrot, or the Grimms.

William Jansen, a leading American folklorist, contributed to the view of folklore as a group's possession. Jansen (1965) gives a theoretical approach to ethnic folklore in which a group's folklore about itself (esoteric) can be distinguished from a group's folklore about another group (exoteric). Using Jansen's concepts, I will give examples of folklore that I have collected from Chira, Costa Rica and New Orleans, Louisiana, to illustrate what is perhaps a universal characteristic of ethnocentrism: the use of esoteric and exoteric folklore as boundary maintaining devices.

The island of Chira, Costa Rica, is inhabited by two groups: Guanacastecos, a Ladino population that has preserved many Meso-American cultural elements in combination with elements derived from colonial Spanish culture, and Josefinos, non-Ladino migrants from the central highlands of Costa Rica, whose culture is primarily derived from colonial Spanish sources with borrowing from local Ladino culture. Both groups are undergoing acculturation, and it is anticipated that eventually the differences between the groups will be primarily in terms of physical characteristics. Indeed, the groups already have many behavioral practices in common, such as the adherence to the hot-cold system of medical practices (Orso 1970). Nevertheless informants insist that there are basic differences between the two groups. These differences are preserved in what would be generally considered cultural stereotypes and superstitions. The following are examples taken from my field notes:

Guanacasteco Esoteric Folklore. Guanacastecos are black and "hot," and are better suited to live in the hot climate of the island. Guanacastecos are quick tempered and are good fighters. The western part of the island where most of the natives live is the most healthy and pleasant part of Chira.

Guanacasteco Exoteric Folklore. Josefinos are white and "cold," and are not suited for Chira. Josefinos with light colored eyes are "cats" that can see in the dark. Two Josefino female schoolteachers were *mariconas* (homosexuals or sissies) because they could not take married life and left their husbands. Josefinos are not good fighters.

Josefino Esoteric Folklore. The Josefino *patrón* of Chira came to the island thirty-five years ago with only one hundred *pesos* and two cows, and built up a fortune in cattle ranching and salt production. The *patrón* paid for the funeral of a poor Guanacasteco employee whose ghost returned to thank him (the traditional folklore motif of the grateful dead). Josefinos are industrious and hard working and built the school and the Catholic church in Chira.

Josefino Exoteric Folklore. There are two old Guanacasteca women on the island who are witches, and most natives know how to practice sorcery. Natives live in sin and adultery and are lazy and poor because they don't want to work. Natives are like Indians because they like to drink too much, and they go crazy when they are drunk.

The Feast of Saint Joseph in New Orleans, Louisiana (Orso 1972). Saint Joseph's day, March 19, usually falls within the Catholic Lenten period. Classifying it as a holy day of obligation, the church suspends the normal Lenten restrictions for that day. In the nineteenth century in New Orleans, French Catholics celebrated Saint Joseph's day, or *Micarême*, with masquerade balls, dances, weddings, and parties. New Orleans blacks, many of them Catholics, also celebrated the day and continue to do so with the appearance of the black Mardi Gras "Indian" tribes singing and dancing on the streets of the city on the evening of March 19. In the early twentieth century, Arbreshe Italians (originally of Albania and later of Sicily) began celebrating Saint Joseph's day with private feasts and with eastern Mediterranean-style home altars laden with food, flowers, and religious objects that were open for public viewing. By the late 1940s, the custom of building Saint Joseph day altars had diffused to other Italians and even to black Spiritualist churches. By 1967 the Italian Cultural Society of New Orleans began sponsoring a large outdoor altar at Saint Joseph's church and an annual parade through the downtown area of the city on Saint Joseph's day. Since the Italian parade normally follows by only two days the Irish Saint Patrick's day parade of March 17, this seems to be the conscious use of esoteric folklore in Italian ethnic one-upmanship. The Italian parade is much more elaborate and expensive than the Irish and demonstrates to all New Orleanians that Italians today are more prosperous than the Irish who discriminated against Italian "Dagos" in the beginning of the present century. Thus the Italian Cultural Society has chosen a day that has traditionally been important to French Catholics, blacks, and Arbreshe Italians as the day to promote esoteric Italian ethnic identity.

The use of ethnic folklore to increase ethnic identity can lead to an overemphasis of ethnocentrism. This may be illustrated by an example from Claude Lévi-Strauss. In dealing with the illusion of totemism, Lévi-Strauss (1962, 1963a) theorizes that through two transformations (or logical shifts) from a pure totemic structure, a caste-type society is obtained in which groups of people become so identified with their own emblem (or folklore) that they cannot exchange women.

Ethnic folklore studies are a necessary first step in the goal of discovering universal folklore motifs.

The Universal Folklorists. The first person to give emphasis to the idea of the psychic unity of mankind was Sir Edward Burnett Tylor. Through his efforts the notion gained wide acceptance for a time in England and elsewhere. Tylor, a unilinear evolutionist, was overwhelmed with the regularity of the grand movement or evolution of culture from savagery to barbarism to civilization, and as Harris (1968:173-175) points out, it mattered not at all to Tylor if the widespread similarities in cultural development were the result of independent invention or of diffusion, since either or both substantiated his idea of psychic unity.

Tylor seems to have become convinced of the psychic unity of mankind through his comparative study of myth. In 1865 in *Researches into the Early History of Mankind,* Tylor (1964) first treated the myths of observation. In these myths he showed that people the world over upon discovering the remains of boats on mountaintops or great bones buried in the earth have created stories of races of giant men or monsters who lived in the past and who were destroyed by a great flood. For Tylor (1964:167), these myths resulted from the identical workings of the human mind in similar situations. In a subsequent chapter on the geographical distribution of myths, Tylor (1964:193-194) stated that one can find primitive myths identical in character to the myths from classic Indian civilization deriving from the great Aryan race. Tylor accepted the then popular views of the English solar mythologists, such as Müller and Kuhn, that myths originated from the contemplation of nature.[4] The theories of the solar mythologists were challenged and finally defeated by a student of Tylor, Andrew Lang. Yet all of these men accepted the idea of the psychic unity of mankind, and in this sense they were all universal folklorists. All would agree with Tylor (1964:194) that "it is not needful to accumulate great masses of such tales as these in order to show that the myth-making facility belongs to mankind in general, and manifests itself in the most distant region, where its unity of principle develops itself in endless variety and form."

Tylor (1958) also used folklore in another sense to substantiate his theory of unilinear evolution and collected examples of folklore from his contemporary Englishmen to document his concept of survivals. He used children's games, proverbs, and other customs as examples of survivals. For Tylor (1958:89), proverbs had survived from the period of Upper Savagery when they were useful devices in popular education. Tylor also believed that it was the task of anthropology (the reformer's science) to help eliminate many useless and perhaps harmful superstitions found in folklore.

Sir James Frazer, another Victorian anthropologist, contributed to universal folklore with his monumental *The Golden Bough* (1935) and other works on folklore. From the masses of documents he collected, Frazer also concluded that there was an essential similarity in the working of the human mind.

As mentioned previously the Finnish method of comparative folklore research began in the late nineteenth century with the work of Julius Krohn. Today the Finnish method remains one of the most significant approaches in universal folkloristics.[5] After 1900 Finnish folklorists continued to make significant contributions to universal folklore. In 1910 Antti Aarne published the first index of European folktale types. This index went beyond narrow ethnic and national boundaries and showed that the same folktales, with minor variations, were told in many parts of the world. The index was expanded by Stith Thompson in 1928 and again in 1961, and today is an indispensable tool for the folktale researcher (Aarne and Thompson 1964). The most significant contribution to the universal folklore approach is the monumental six-volume *Motif Index of Folk Literature* by Stith Thompson (1932-36). In the *Index* small elements of folklore, called motifs, are arranged by topic, and the entire work is indexed in the last volume. The *Index* can be used to identify a superstition, folktale, legend, etc., and determine in what other parts of the world the item has been recorded.[6]

Paulo de Carvalho-Neto (1972:22-23) traces the origin of psychoanalytical folklore to three obscure nineteenth-century European scholars—Laistner, Clodd, and Golther—who argued that folklore was the product of nightmares. However, Sigmund Freud is generally credited with the creation of a psychoanalytical folklore theory, the interpretive approach most disliked by orthodox American folklorists (Dorson 1963:105). Freud attempted to establish an analogy between dreams and myths, since both used oneiric symbols. These symbols "are not the exclusive property of the dreamer. They are a type of subconscious collective patrimony which is verifiable in the plebeian psyche, in myths, in legends, and in proverbs. The symbolism . . . results from the accumulated experience of generations . . . and is revealed more intelligibly in folklore" (Carvalho-Neto 1972: 23). According to Freud and Oppenheim, it is

very much more convenient to study dream symbolism in folklore
than in actual dreams. Dreams are obliged to conceal things and only
surrender their secrets to interpretation; . . . comic anecdotes which
are disguised as dreams are intended as communications, meant to give
pleasure to the person who tells them as well as to the listener. . . .
These stories delight in stripping off the veiling symbols. In the following
quatrain, [sung in Bavarian and Austrian mountain districts] . . . the
penis appears as a scepter:

> Last night I dreamt
> I was King of the Land,
> And how jolly I was
> With a prick in my hand.

Now compare with this "dream" the following example [from the
Austrian Alps] . . . in which the same symbolism is employed outside a
dream:

> I love a little lass
> The prettiest I've ever seen,
> I'll put a scepter in your hand
> And you shall be a queen.
>   (Freud and Oppenheim 1958:27)

It was perhaps Freud's insistence upon the universality of the
sexual symbolism in folklore and dreams (based on the assumption
of the collective subconscious and the psychic unity of mankind)
that caused his rejection by American scholars.[7]

In 1913 Carl Jung severed his intellectual relations with Freud
and established his own school of analytical psychology in Switzer-
land. The Jungians also consider folklore as an important part of
their training, and students of the Jung Institute must be trained in
the psychological interpretation of fairy tales (Dorson 1963:107).
According to Jung all mythical characters correspond to inner
psychic experiences and originally derive from them. For example
the trickster, a universal folklore figure, is considered by Jung
(1956:195-200) to be a "psychologem," or a very ancient and archetypal psychic structure. Jung believed that there were ever present
elements in the unconscious psyche of mankind that kept repro-
ducing similar myths and myth elements (archetypes). Jung felt
that primitive man had not invented myths but rather had experienced
them as revelations of the preconscious psyche. Since modern man
shares a collective unconscious, he also reexperiences the archetypal
revelations. Obviously Jung was a universal folklorist who accepted
the idea of psychic unity.

In 1927 the American anthropologist Paul Radin made an im-
portant contribution to the universal approach in his book, *Primitive
Man as Philosopher*. Written primarily as a challenge to Lévy-
Bruhl's idea of a prelogical mentality among primitives, Radin (1957:

xxi) used aboriginal folklore to prove that all human groups have contained individuals who because of their temperaments and interests were philosophical thinkers. In arguing that there were basically two types of men, the man of action and the philosopher, Radin gave support to the theory of psychic unity. Most of his proof came from folklore, which he considered to be the creation of men of philosophy.

Today Claude Lévi-Strauss is the leading advocate of the universal folklore approach in anthropology and folklore. Lévi-Strauss has concentrated primarily on the study of myth to document his theory of the structural basis of human thought, behavior, and culture. He seeks to demonstrate that the structure of the human mind is essentially the same everywhere and that it has a certain nature or quality (Hammel 1972:3). He proposes a method of myth analysis that allows us to understand some basic logical processes that are at the heart of mythical thought. In all myths there is a progression from the awareness of oppositions (such as earth and sky) to their resolution or mediation (Lévi-Strauss 1963b:224). In deciphering the universal code of myths Lévi-Strauss demonstrates that people everywhere have used myths to order their perception of the world that they live in. Structuralism now appears to be one of the dominant theoretical approaches in European folklore, and it has been well received by American anthropologists and folklorists. For example Sarah Blaffer (1972) analyzes the folklore of the Tzotzil Indians of Chiapas, Mexico in an excellent application of the structural methodology and substantiates Lévi-Strauss's claim of the universality of mythical thought processes.

Alan Lomax (1968), an American ethnomusicologist, in his *Folk Song Style and Culture* explains his methods for the cross-cultural comparison of music and song style and gives some of the results of his studies. In his search for universals of song and music, Lomax has determined that song style symbolizes and reinforces some important elements of social structure in all cultures. For example he found that vocal stance always varies with the severity of sexual restrictions for women in all parts of the world (Lomax 1968:vii-viii). For the first time, Lomax discovered predictable and universal relationships between social structure and culture pattern, and expressive and communicative processes.

Whereas esoteric and exoteric folklore have probably been used for thousands of years to reinforce ethnocentrism and maintain group boundaries, the scholarly use of applied folklore to promote ethnic identity began in Finland in the seventeenth century. Ironically folklore also was used by the British unilinear evolutionists in the nineteenth century to prove the psychic unity of mankind and panhuman identity. In Finland the emphasis on ethnic identity evolved to the promotion of panhuman identity through the efforts of Julius Krohn and Antti Aarne.

As Dorson (1963:96) has implied, these two different approaches to cultural identity through folklore need not be in opposition and can be complementary. Yet with the exception of the Finnish folklorists, who maintain a balance of the two approaches, most scholars in the present century have concentrated on one of the two types of identity. Anthropology and folklore can serve two masters, and there is no inconsistency in equally emphasizing panhuman and ethnic identities.

It is absolutely essential to collect and study the ethnic folklore of all cultures because it is only through the cross-cultural comparison of ethnic folklores that universal patterns and motifs emerge. Promotion of the awareness of panhuman identity through the teaching of universal folklore seems a worthy goal for both anthropologists and folklorists today.

NOTES

1. I wish to acknowledge the helpful criticisms of an early draft of this paper by Dr. Malcolm Webb and Dr. Frank deCaro.

2. Professor William Wilson has kindly granted permission to quote material from his working papers on the history of European folklore scholarship.

3. The name of this organization is somewhat misleading in English. Upon its foundation in 1831 by twelve young teachers and graduates of Helsinki University, the purpose was to publish the folklore material collected by Elias Lönnrot. Today the primary tasks of the society are to promote research in national culture, to maintain and enlarge the central folklore archive and a national library, and to publish scientific literature and various periodicals, such as *Proverbium*.

4. Müller and Kuhn were also convinced (following linguistic studies and such evidence as Grimm's Law of 1822) that myths originated in India in the proto-Indo-European ancestor language and diffused to the rest of the world (Dorson 1965). Tylor (1964) seemed to accept this idea of diffusion from India. In his *Researches* . . . he related eight myth themes found in American Indian folklore to their Asiatic (Aryan) prototypes. To Tylor the diffusion of a myth theme demonstrated psychic unity as well as proof that two similar myths had independent origin. It remained for a student of Tylor, Andrew Lang, to challenge the narrow interpretations of the solar mythologists like Müller and Kuhn who treated all myth elements as symbols of the sun, moon, lightning, etc. Lang's success probably contributed to the end of interest in folklore research in England (Dorson 1965:83).

5. For an explanation of this method, see Dundes 1965:414-416.

6. Each motif is assigned a motif number, such as E341 for the grateful dead, and the system is flexible to allow the assignment of additional numbers

as new motifs are recorded. Today the *Index* needs expansion to include more examples of non-Western folklore, and revision to include new information on the presence of motifs in countries other than originally recorded by Thompson, or the diffusion of motifs to additional countries.

7. Space does not permit an evaluation of the controversy regarding Freud's sexual symbolism, which I feel no obligation to defend. It is of interest, however, that American folklorists have been led to their present overemphasis of ethnic folklore studies by rejecting the Finnish method (too much work for too little results) and the psychoanalytical approach ("trash," "absurd," and "fantastic") (Dorson 1963:108). However, some American folklorists have shown a positive response to Lévi-Strauss's structural (universal) approach.

REFERENCES

Aarne, Antti, and Stith Thompson, 1964. *The Types of the Folktale* (Helsinki: Finnish Scientific Academy).

Bauman, Richard, 1972. Differential Identity and the Social Base of Folklore. In *Toward New Perspectives in Folklore*, Américo Paredes and Richard Bauman, eds. (Austin: University of Texas Press), pp. 31-41.

Blaffer, Sarah, 1972. *The Black-Man of Zinacantan* (Austin: University of Texas Press).

Brunvand, Jan, 1968. *The Study of American Folklore* (New York: W. W. Norton).

Carvalho-Neto, Paulo de, 1972. *Folklore and Psychoanalysis* (Miami: University of Miami Press).

Dorson, Richard, 1963. Current Folklore Theories. *Current Anthropology* 4:93-110.

———— 1965. The Eclipse of Solar Mythology. In *The Study of Folklore*, Alan Dundes, ed. (Englewood Cliffs, N. J.: Prentice-Hall), pp. 57-83.

———— 1972. *Folklore and Folklife* (Chicago: University of Chicago Press).

Dundes, Alan, ed., 1965. *The Study of Folklore* (Englewood Cliffs, N. J.: Prentice-Hall).

Frazer, Sir James, 1935. *The Golden Bough* (New York: The Macmillan Co.). (First published in 1890.)

Freud, Sigmund, and D. E. Oppenheim, 1958. *Dreams in Folklore* (New York: International Universities Press).

Hammel, Eugene A., 1972. *The Myth of Structural Analysis: Lévi-Strauss and the Three Bears*, Addison-Wesley Modular Publications, Module No. 25 (Reading, Mass.: Addison-Wesley).

Harris, Marvin, 1968. *The Rise of Anthropological Theory* (New York: Thomas Y. Crowell).

Jansen, William H., 1965. The Esoteric-Exoteric Factor in Folklore. In *The Study of Folklore*, Allan Dundes, ed. (Englewood Cliffs, N. J.: Prentice-Hall), pp. 43-51.

Jung, Carl G., 1956. On the Psychology of the Trickster Figure. In *The Trickster*, Paul Radin, ed. (New York: Philosophical Library), pp. 195-211.

Krohn, Kaarle, 1971. *Folklore Methodology* (Austin: University of Texas Press).

Kroeber, A. L., and Clyde Kluckhohn, 1963. *Culture* (New York: Random House).

Lévi-Strauss, Claude, 1962. *The Savage Mind* (Chicago: University of Chicago Press).

———— 1963a. *Totemism* (Boston: Beacon Press).

———— 1963b. *Structural Anthropology* (New York: Basic Books).

Lomax, Alan, 1968. *Folk Song Style and Culture*, American Association for the Advancement of Science, Publication No. 88 (Washington, D. C.).

Orso, Ethelyn, 1970. *Hot and Cold in the Folk Medicine of the Island of Chira, Costa Rica,* Dissertation and Monograph Series, No. 1 (Baton Rouge: Latin American Studies Institute of Louisiana State University).

———— 1972. The Feast of Saint Joseph in New Orleans. (Paper presented at the annual meeting of the American Folklore Society in Austin, Texas.)

Radin, Paul, 1957. *Primitive Man as Philosopher* (New York: Dover Publications). (First published in 1927.)

Taylor, Archer, 1961. Characteristics of German Folklore Studies. *The Journal of American Folklore* 74:293-301.

Thompson, Stith, 1932-36. *The Motif Index of Folk Literature* (Bloomington: Indiana University Press).

Tylor, Sir Edward, 1958. *The Origins of Culture* (New York: Harper Torchbooks). (First published in 1871 as Chapters I-X of *Primitive Culture.*)

———— 1964. *Researches Into the Early History of Mankind* (Chicago: University of Chicago Press). (First published in 1865.)

Wallace, Anthony F. C., 1956. Revitalization Movements. *American Anthropologist* 58:264-281.

Wilson, William, 1967. Herder, Folklore, and Romantic Nationalism. (Paper presented at the annual meeting of the American Folklore Society in Toronto, Canada.)

———— 1972. Folklore and Nationalism in Finland. (Paper presented at the annual meeting of the American Folklore Society in Austin, Texas.)

Entertainment and Black Identity in Bermuda

FRANK E. MANNING

IN Bermuda, a circum-Caribbean British colony with fifty-five thousand inhabitants, there is a wide spectrum of clubs.[1] A few of these have been the private preserve of the "Forty Thieves," a white merchant aristocracy which has run Bermuda for three and a half centuries. Less privileged whites have also built a number of clubs, distinguished chiefly by social class and ethnicity. All white clubs, though, have held one policy in common: racial segregation.[2] Like other white institutions in Bermuda, they have excluded blacks, who comprise three-fifths of the resident population and nearly four-fifths of the native-born population (Census of Bermuda 1970).

Bermudian blacks responded to segregation by forming their own clubs, chiefly for sports and recreation but more recently for charitable work, horticulture, haute couture fashion, and artistic enterprises. Within these clubs symbols of racial-cultural identity have always been present—hardly surprising in view of the conditions prevailing in Bermudian society. In recent years, however, these symbols have become more numerous and more pronounced, corresponding to sociopolitical gains achieved by blacks in Bermuda as well as to their growing acquaintance with black nationalism in the West Indies and with various aspects of the black movement in the United States. I will deal with the symbolization of racial-cultural identity within the context of entertainment productions sponsored on a regular basis by fourteen black sports and recreational clubs licensed to serve liquor.[3] The productions I will discuss include stage shows, dances, "cocktail sips," talent and beauty competitions, parties, fashion shows, fairs, and festivals. My remarks will focus on the hermeneutics of entertainment symbolism, on the identity transition which I believe this symbolism encourages, and on the sociocultural context within which the transition is taking place.

Symbolic expressions of racial-cultural identity extrapolated from club entertainment events can be put into two broad categories: Afro-American symbols and Afro-Caribbean symbols. The former group is drawn primarily from the revitalized black heritage in the United States. The latter group has its source in West Indian public performances. Let us look first at the Afro-American category, which is divisible into soul, black mod, and Afro symbols.

Soul Symbols. Bermudians customarily describe the music that is played, sung, and danced to at the clubs as "soul"—a genre that has been called the music of the people (Keil, 1966:32) and that for present purposes includes the earlier blues styles as well as the newer "funky beat." The sounds of Isaac Hayes, Lou Donaldson, James Brown, Junior Walker and the All Stars, the Metermen, the Supremes, Roberta Flack, Aretha Franklin, Nina Simone and Nancy Wilson have all enjoyed wide appeal in the clubs, as has more recently the music of Al Green, the Chi-Lites, the Temptations, Gladys Knight and the Pips, the Jackson Five, and many others. Bermudian singers and musicians build much of their repertoire on the recordings of these artists, which generally attain popularity in Bermuda within several weeks after release in the United States.

Soul, however, is more than just music. Although a difficult symbol to define or even describe, it is clearly, among other things, a badge of identity, an expression of a life style, a criterion of what is considered authentically black, and a summation of the conscious understandings and shared sensitivities of a people (Keil, 1966:164-190). Hannerz (1970:16) has simplified these various meanings by calling soul a shorthand symbol of the black "national character." It can be said that soul is the catalyst of a definitional transformation. An ethos which has long been the object of moral condemnation by whites and self-deprecation by blacks is defined as soul and assumes a new, positive meaning.

Black Mod Symbols. While soul refers specifically to music and more generally to an entire ethos, black mod refers to a mode of dress but also conveys an expression of racial identity. The black mod look is especially popular among men at club entertainment events, although women also sport it. Men's fashions include striped bell-bottom pants, two-tone pants, pink, yellow, or purple silk shirts, bolero shirts, ruffled shirts, see-through knit shirts, suede fringed vests, jump suits, paisley scarves, and neckties made of floral and psychedelic prints. Traditional Western style suits are also worn but usually are cut and tailored along mod lines. Mod fashions sported by women include striped bell-bottom slacks, two-tone slacks, bubble blouses, wool knit skirts and jerseys, leather collars, suede fringed handbags, chain belts, large round earrings, gold bracelets, colorful scarves, and pink and yellow tinted sunglasses.

Afro Symbols. The most fashionable Afro symbols among clubgoers of both sexes are Afro coiffures, dashiki clothing, and jewelry made of beads or carved wood chips. African print dresses, turbans, and robes are also worn occasionally by women. These symbols are close in meaning to soul and black mod symbols but, unlike the latter, refer primarily to a historical heritage rather than a contemporary life style. The Afro concept is thus the cultural matrix of the black ethos, relating it to a larger setting and tradition.

Let us now consider the Afro-Caribbean symbolic category, which consists of creole, carnival, and Gombey symbols.

Creole Symbols. The term *creole* is used here in the sense which it originally had in the West Indies—as a designation for cultural forms developed in the Caribbean and distinctive of that area but with traceable or at least plausible African ancestry (cf. Mintz, 1967:147n). Calypso, reggae, and spouge music, together with the use of instruments such as bongos and maracas, are the major creole forms that have found their way into the repertoire of Bermudian performers. Although a year or two often elapse between a song's release in the West Indies and its rise to popularity in Bermuda (considerably longer than in the case of American soul music), Caribbean creole music enjoys a large Bermudian following.

Carnival Symbols. The growing appeal of Afro-Caribbean cultural forms has prompted one club to organize an annual visit from representatives of the Trinidadian Carnival. It is held concurrently with Cup Match, a club-sponsored cricket rivalry and the main indigenous festival in Bermuda. Carnival events include steel band performances, "jump-up" dances in which spectators join performers on stage, parades of costumed troupes playing '*mas*, and Calypso King and Carnival Queen contests. Bermudians are encouraged to enter Carnival competitions, and those who win travel to the West Indies to participate in Caribbean festivals.

Gombey Symbols. The Gombey Dance is a complex mimetic performance which syncretizes African, West Indian, and Amerindian (as well as Christian, British, and possibly Spanish) elements, but which in its present form is uniquely Bermudian. Troupes comprised of both children and adults dress in elaborate costumes symbolizing the above cultural themes and disguise their faces to keep secret their personal identities. They dance to the accompaniment of drums, fifes, snares, whistles, and cracking whips. Clubs engage the troupes to perform at fairs, festivals, and sports events.

In addition to symbols of racial-cultural identity club entertainment events are also replete with what I call symbols of "tone," i.e., symbols which emphasize form over substance or content and which have to do primarily with pedigree, mood, and demeanor rather than with identity. Three types of tonal symbols are especially relevant to this discussion: symbols of elegance, symbols of sexuality, and symbols of exuberance. Let me briefly review these tonal symbols.

Symbols of Elegance. Symbols of elegance at club entertainment events are conveyed by the setting, clothing fashions, and patterns of sociability. The setting for indoor events includes the lounges, cocktail bars, and cabarets, all of which most clubs have recently built or remodelled at costs approaching $100,000. Decor and furnishings are lavish and clearly stylized along the lines of Bermuda's luxury hotels. At outdoor events special decorations convey an image of luxury consistent with that of the indoor setting. Clothing styles sported by the people complement the opulence of the physical surroundings. Black mod and Afro fashions do not come cheap, and clubgoers are therefore good customers at Bermuda's most expensive boutiques. Patterns of sociability include drinking the most expensive brands of liquor (Scotch is the popular favorite in most clubs) and generously buying drinks for one's friends. The overall image of extravagance is boosted by the hiring of disc jockeys to play records while the band is taking breaks. In sum the symbolic atmosphere at club events is one of elegance, glamour, high style, and a kind of Veblenesque conspicuous consumption.

Symbols of Sexuality. Symbols of sexuality are also prominently displayed at club entertainment events. In addition to projecting the mod and Afro images, women's fashions are designed to enhance sex appeal. Flesh-clinging dresses with plunging necklines, miniskirts which suggestively expose the thighs, two-piece ensembles which daringly bare the midriff, hot pants outfits which accentuate the pubes, hips, and buttocks, and tight-fitting pants suits which gloriously contour the cantilevered dimensions of their wearers are popular attire. Similarly the expensive fashions worn by men, together with their extravagant spending, would seem to enlarge their image of sexual prowess. To appropriate an American comparison, they fit Keil's (1966:26) description of what blacks commonly call a "no good man"—one who "spends his money freely, dresses well, and is great in bed."

Many dances entail a variety of sexually suggestive gestures, and the lyrics of popular songs—especially calypso and reggae music—are often liberally spiced with double entendres about sexual organs and acts as well as situations involving adulterous liaisons. The latter theme also articulates a social characteristic of the club audience. Although an equal ratio of men and women attend club events, few of them are married couples. Men are reluctant to bring their wives to the club, and I gather the strong impression that a majority of the women who attend are either single, separated, or divorced. The club ethos attaches no stigma to extramarital relationships. In fact such relationships are expected and often joked about, both in the conversation of the audience and in the songs they relish.

Symbols of Exuberance. Symbols of exuberance emphasize primarily youth and youthful attitudes. Talent and beauty competitions for youth are promoted periodically, and one club arranges for Miss Americolor to be guest model at an annual "vogue evening" of fashion, cocktails, and dancing. Many clubs also sponsor local entrants in the Miss Bermuda Pageant, who are usually chosen from among the models at club events.

Young entertainers are idolized by the older generation as well as their peers. Middle-aged clubgoers often poke derisive fun at entertainers of their own age, referring to them as fuddyduddys and old-timers but, in general, respond enthusiastically to the younger and more soulful groups. Listening to these young performers they make comments such as "Man, he's really saying something," or "That's some kind of show, isn't it?"

Clubgoers of all ages participate eagerly in the most strenuous dances performed by youth, including such favorites as the Cissy Strut, the Popcorn, the Chicken, the Bird, and the Donkey. The only time I saw the middle-aged segment refrain from these dances was when an undertaker was present and passing out his business cards.

Having summarily presented the component symbols of entertainment, let us now rejoin them to the setting from which they were taken. As is readily apparent from the previous discussion, symbols of identity and tone are closely interconnected in display and usage. They share the same contexts of form (clothing, coiffure, jewelry, music) and action (dances, sociability styles), as well as the same overall ethos. In view of this physical and operational integration, what meanings and motivations are conveyed by the symbolic gestalt of entertainment productions?

An answer may begin to emerge when we look at an axial figure such as the songstress, fashion model, or beauty contestant. Mod styled, Afro-coiffured, luxuriantly bejewelled, sensually arousing, and youthfully zestful, she simultaneously displays the symbols of racial-cultural identity and those of elegance, sexuality, and exuberance. Moreover, by physically associating these symbols, she also associates the meanings which they elicit; the symbolic conjoinment of black identity and elegant sensuality suggests a conceptual relationship.

The titillating black female thus exemplifies a principle which Turner (1964:30) calls "polarization of meaning." Dominant symbols, he contends, have both sensory and ideological poles of meaning. Around the sensory pole are clustered meanings that are "frankly, even flagrantly, physiological" and which arouse desire and feeling, whereas around the ideological pole are clustered meanings which refer to norms and values (Turner 1964:31). In the action situation there is an interchange of qualities between the two poles of meaning, charging norms and values with emotion, and ennobling emotion with social legitimacy. Following this postulate, we can say that the sensuously clad, Afro-coiffured young woman interchanges the two responses which she evokes: black identity and prurient passion.

On the male side, the symbolism of a figure such as the singer, musician, or master of ceremonies also associates racial-cultural and tonal forms. His overall performance, together with the energy and commitment with which he renders it, is consciously intended and clearly recognized as soul. His clothing and accessories transmit black mod symbolism as well as a look of affluence and high style. His haircut and perhaps other aspects of his presence express the African heritage. His general appearance and deportment project youthful vigor and sexual prowess. In the action context, all of these symbols are clustered and their meanings interrelated.

From these examples we can see a mutual association of meanings. One aspect of the hermeneutic exchange enhances black identity by investing it with stylistic glamor and sensual appeal. The reciprocal aspect relates elegance, beauty, and youthful dynamism to black people in a black setting, thereby suggesting that these allurements are to be classified in a frame of reference that is black.

The association of racial-cultural and tonal meanings, moreover, is not limited to symbolic action on stage. The lionization of performers makes them culture heroes and role models for their public—here, the club audience. Thus the symbols of clothing, coiffure, and action style seen on stage are also displayed by the spectators. Accordingly clubgoers not only view the symbolic process through which black identity and hedonistic glamour are interrelated but also participate in it by emulating and empathizing with entertainers.

The matter of audience participation raises another relevant consideration. The collective role of the club audience supports and complements the role of the performer. Spectators mimic the entertainer's histrionic gestures and convey their appreciation with shouts of "Heavy, heavy!" "Sing it, baby!" "Yea, man!" "Do your thing, baby!" and the like. This form of response is unmistakably similar to that which is so familiar in Bermuda's black churches where the congregation participates in the preacher's gestural dramatics and expresses its agreement with shouts of "Amen!" "Preach, pastor, preach!" "It's the truth!" "Carry him through, Jesus!" and so forth.

The homology between church ritual and club entertainment derives its present significance from their normative antithesis. Black Christianity in Bermuda is ascetic and fundamentalist and thus severely opposes the hedonistic activities promoted by the clubs, of which the entertainment is the most flagrant example. Accordingly persons do not belong to club and church at the same time in their lives, a situation which makes clubgoers the acknowledged backsliders of Bermuda. Yet most persons in the club continue to hold basic Christian beliefs, have poignant memories of Sunday School, and hope to be saved and return to their church in the future. In the meantime, entertainment, with its ritual-like formal and structural qualities, is imbued with an emotional resonance which adds to its communicative effectiveness by stirring some of the deepest sensitivities of the people.

Perhaps in one respect entertainment has a communicative advantage over religion. As Peacock (1968:243-245) has observed, aesthetic influences may be more powerful than religious ones because aesthetic influences are generally unrecognized, and therefore people are not on guard against them. This principle applies to the present case. The clubs run their dances, shows, fairs, and festivals for recreation, not enculturation. The audience comes to be entertained, not instructed or persuaded. Unprepared for an ideological message, the club audience may be more receptive to one than a religious congregation which expects a message and is therefore ready to question and criticize it.

This reasoning may also help to explain why the colonial government, despite taking severe reprisals against black preachers who have addressed the gospel to social and especially racial issues, has generally been lenient toward the clubs. For example the club liquor license is kept relatively inexpensive and the clubs are allowed to remain open twenty-four hours a day, 364 days a year. (Most clubs have chosen Christmas as the day to close and otherwise are open about eighteen hours daily.) Likewise, although the clubs are legally restricted from selling liquor to nonmembers, allowing nonmembers on the premises after one A.M., and letting anyone visit the club more than three times without joining, these restrictions were never enforced while I was in Bermuda. This type of leniency strongly suggests that the white-controlled power structure views the clubs principally as valuable clients for white-owned liquor businesses, banks, and construction firms, not as communicators of a positive black identity.

Entertainment enjoys a further advantage which makes it a suitable vehicle for expressions of black identity, especially those formulated by Afro-American symbolism. As Keil (1966:16) has commented, entertainment is the one area of black American life which has not been diluted or disfigured by white influences. It has retained its cultural integrity in the face of oppression and continues to bear the marks of its African ancestry. Thus when the modern entertainer consciously covers himself with the symbols of black identity and strives to project the image of a soulman, he is not striking a synthetic pose. He is, rather, articulating a tradition which he and his medium authentically represent.

My contention thus far, then, is twofold: first, that entertainment forges meaningful associations between the symbols of racial-cultural identity and the symbols of tone, an exchange which serves to stylize and sensualize black identity as well as to relate elegance, beauty, and hedonistic glamour to a black social setting; second, that the ritualistic aspects of entertainment, together with its overall aesthetic form, make it an especially appropriate and effective medium to convey black identity.

But if club entertainment communicates and enhances a recognizable version of identity, where does this identity fit in relation to the wider Bermudian society and its cultural traditions? This question can best be answered by looking at two orders of meaning conveyed by identity symbolism. The first order, which has been examined in the course of this article, pertains to the ethos, aesthetics, and tradition of Afro-American and Afro-Caribbean peoples. The second order is more difficult to verbalize but is partially expressed by Fanon's (1967) notion of "black consciousness": the positive awareness among peoples of African ancestry of their heritage and human dignity. Yet the word *black* has gained both conceptual significance and emotional impact since Fanon's writing. It no longer represents merely a generic identification. Through its color referent it has come to symbolize both diametric opposition to white and complete independence from it. Its usage to the exclusion of other terms designating Negroid peoples has become itself an expression of racial pride; conversely, its nonusage is synonymous to living mentally in a white world. James Brown's song, "Say It Loud, I'm Black and I'm Proud," summarizes the meaning that has developed. The two terms—*black* and *proud*—have come to imply each other in the racial context.

As concrete, consciously understood embodiments of this modern sense of blackness, the symbols of identity conveyed through entertainment issue their second order of meaning: racial pride and independence. These symbols, then, work not only to elicit a sense of cultural rapport with Afro-American and Afro-Caribbean peoples, but also to evoke an emotionally-charged allegiance to the black race and a deep feeling of self-esteem in belonging to it.

The significance of these two orders of meaning becomes apparent when we look at the Bermudian folk tradition, which confers on nonwhites the designation of "colored Bermudians," and carefully stipulates that they are separate and superior to peoples of their pigmentation in other parts of the world—especially Americans and West Indians. The folk identity has been preserved in modern times by the white oligarchy and the racially-mixed colonial bourgeoisie, who together exert a powerful influence over much of the information disseminated in Bermuda. For example an amateur historian whose writings are used in Bermudian schools once told me, "The colored people here are clearly superior to those in the United States. After all, they have 350 years of British culture behind them." West Indians are recognized as sharing in this hallowed British heritage, but not nearly as fully as Bermudians. Accordingly, West Indians are stereotyped as belligerent, uncouth, and stupid—attributes which make them only slightly better than the American Negro. Thus when a Bermudian runs afoul of the political-economic establishment, he is often denigrated with the charge of having "West Indian blood in his veins."

The extent to which Bermudians have traditionally eschewed any identification as black can be gleaned from the recollections of a West Indian who taught in Bermuda (Scott, 1969). He recalled that when he first arrived in Bermuda in the 1930s he referred to himself as black and was promptly and adamantly corrected by his sixth-standard students, who assured him that he was not black but "chocolate brown." Making further inquiries he learned that the students also distinguished three other shades of brown, the lightest of which was "tantalizing brown." Beyond the browns there was another shade, "high yellow."

For reasons such as this, symbolic expressions which invite the club audience to identify as black have more than merely semantic significance. These symbols encourage the audience to put aside their particularistic identity as colored Bermudians and to adopt a more universal identification which relates them to other peoples of African ancestry on the basis of common ethnicity, common experiences stemming from colonialism and slavery, and a common cultural heritage which has been rediscovered and revitalized in recent years. Or to phrase it differently, the identity conveyed through entertainment moves the club audience from an insular society where they are known and socially valued by the degree to which their shading approximates the white ideal, toward a cosmopolitan black world where shared symbols and sensitivities form the basis of a cultural order independent of white standards.

This does not mean, however, that we should expect clubgoers to enter a show as "colored" and leave as "black." While an identity may be symbolized in an instant, it is learned slowly and in relation to the social experience of the learner—an experience which in Bermuda is still strongly influenced by conservative forces. The role of entertainment in these circumstances is not to provide a kind of public shock treatment which induces people to adopt a new identity in defiance of restraints and inhibitions. Rather it is to foster a gradual transition of cultural consciousness and to sustain this transition against the social forces which counteract it. Without the role played by entertainment, the concepts and values on which the new black identity is based would be likely to atrophy if they could not immediately be incorporated into daily life. But because these concepts and values are preserved in entertainment symbolism, they can be kept before the minds of the people, gradually internalized, and worked out as conditions allow.

The middle-aged segment of the club audience holds a significant position. As we have seen, the older members are strongly attracted by the youthful image and the symbols of racial-cultural identity related to it even though many of them have not personally mustered the courage to don a dashiki or remove the straightener from their hair. But drawn into empathy with youth and youthful attitudes, they become allies of the new identity rather than opponents of it. They are also inclined to instill it in their own children who are, of course, psychically and socially freer than the parental generation to assimilate a new identity.

What lines of inquiry for other studies are suggested by the Bermudian case? The most obvious, of course, is that aesthetic symbolic action should be given careful analytical attention. Although performed and appreciated for the sake of enjoyment, aesthetic action may convey meanings and motivations that have important social consequences.

But the study of aesthetic symbolism often presents a peculiar difficulty for the anthropologist, especially in complex societies. Because aesthetic symbolism is generally not seen on the conscious level as conveying ethical ideals and imperatives, it does not give rise to goal-oriented organizations. There is no church or political party formed to propagate its creed. Hence the anthropologist studying aesthetic performances usually finds that their devotees do not constitute a circumscribed social group of the kind in which he normally conducts research.

In the Bermudian case, however, the circumstances are somewhat different. The audience is united by an institutional bond; its members constitute a club. They associate not only as spectators and participants at entertainment events, but in a wide range of club activities—sports, games, beneficial and service programs—as well as in daily sociability at the club bar. As the members often say, the club is their second home.

If this combination of symbolic and social features has a wider currency, an approach is opened to the study of voluntary associations different from that customarily employed by anthropologists. As review articles by Banton (1968) and Hammond (1972) point out, associations have been exhaustively typologized; related to systems of status and role differentiation; and examined in terms of their evolution, psychosocial functioning, and place in the economic order. The approach I have taken here asserts that associations may also be viewed as centers of symbolic action where cultural meanings are formulated, shared, and learned.

NOTES

1. A broader and somewhat differently oriented analysis of the material presented in this article is found in chapters 6 and 7 of my book (Manning 1973). The material is used here with permission of Cornell University Press.

Field research was conducted in Bermuda in 1969-70 and 1972. A research grant was awarded by the National Science Foundation (GS-2549) and a stipend given by the Carolina Population Center. I also wish to acknowledge the Institute of Social and Economic Research at Memorial University of Newfoundland, which provided financial assistance for attending the 1973 annual meeting of the Southern Anthropological Society in Wrightsville Beach, North Carolina, where a shortened version of this article was delivered in the key symposium. Finally I am grateful to Heather Batten, who typed and retyped the article for publication.

2. Private clubs were the last bastion of de jure segregation in Bermuda, maintaining their racial barriers until the passage of the Race Relations Act of 1969. Since then segregation has been preserved on a de facto basis. White clubs are at best tokenly integrated, and black clubs remain almost entirely black.

3. The fourteen clubs are collectively known in Bermuda as "workmen's clubs," although only three use the word in their official names.

REFERENCES

Banton, Michael, 1968. Voluntary Associations. In *International Encyclopedia of the Social Sciences*, D. L. Sills, ed. (New York: Macmillan), Vol. 16, pp. 357-362.

Census of Bermuda, 1970. (Hamilton, Bermuda: Government Publication).

Fanon, Franz, 1967. *Black Skin, White Masks*, trans. Charles Markmann (New York: Grove Press).

Hammond, Dorothy, 1972. *Associations* (Reading Mass.: Addison-Wesley Modular Publications).

Hanners, Ulf, 1970. The Significance of Soul. In *Soul*, Lee Rainwater, ed. (Chicago: Aldine), pp. 15-30.

Keil, Charles, 1966. *Urban Blues* (Chicago: University of Chicago Press).

Manning, Frank, 1973. *Black Clubs in Bermuda* (Ithaca: Cornell University Press).

Mintz, Sidney, 1967. Caribbean Nationhood in Anthropological Perspective. In *Caribbean Integration*, Sybil Lewis and Thomas Mathews, eds. (Rio Piedras, P.R.: Institute of Caribbean Studies, University of Puerto Rico), pp. 141-154.

Peacock, James, 1968. *Rites of Modernization* (Chicago: University of Chicago Press).

Scott, V. F., 1969. What Makes Expatriate Teachers Disenchanted. *The Bermuda Sun Weekly*, December 6.

Turner, Victor, 1964. Symbols in Ndembu Ritual. In *Closed Systems and Open Minds*, Max Gluckman, ed. (Chicago: Aldine), pp. 20-51.

Ethnics, Emics, and the New Ideology: The Identity Potential of Indian English

WILLIAM L. LEAP

THE important role which language plays in the maintenance of social and cultural identity has long been recognized in anthropological science.[1] This paper will consider some aspects of the truth of that observation. Documenting various instances where language provides a basis for a people's sense of identity would be useful but would tell us little more about the reality of identity concepts beyond what is already apparent—that identity concepts *can* be formed out of linguistic variables. This paper argues that there is more to a consideration of identity concepts than could be suggested by mere documentation. We recognize, as social scientists, that concepts of identity do not just happen, but like all aspects of human behavior, are created as products of deliberate (i.e. symbolic) design. When a concept of identity is formed, part of the existing cultural inventory is given priority value; it is judged to be the focal point around which other aspects of the life style can be interpreted, validated and legitimized. Documentation could establish, for example, that the Portuguese immigrants of New England view themselves in terms of a "dumb Portguee" ethic, which Smith discusses in her paper elsewhere in this volume (pp. 81-91). Yet Smith also shows how this identity concept serves to maintain the Portuguese immigrants within highly specific segments of the New England wage economy. In that sense the concept guarantees its continuation as a self-fulfilling prophesy; and as long as we view identity concepts strictly within the purview of their identification, our analysis serves only to help that prophesy fulfill itself.

Smith makes the point that I wish to pursue. Concepts of identity must be considered in terms of the consequences of a group's identification. Concepts of identity, as ideological constructs, comment as much on external social forces as they do on the internal ones. For this reason we cannot accept concepts of identity on face value. We need to know why the concept was formed, why it has its particular representation, and what possibilities and preclusions result from this formation.

With this awareness in mind, we will examine a concept of identity currently being developed out of a set of linguistic characteristics. The language in question is Indian English, the variety of American English currently in use within reservation contexts and some urban Indian enclaves in this country. The exploration of the identity potential of Indian English will not only suggest the importance of the question of consequences, but will also point out the kind of scientific responsibility which must accompany any study of group identity. This question of responsibility is discussed in the final section of the paper.

Indian English, one of the numerous English language varieties in use in contemporary America, has only begun to receive systematic research attention; hence, any discussion of this language variety must be based on fragmentary impressions accompanied by varying degrees of empirical support.[2] Because there is a high degree of consensus within these observations, several general comments about the nature of this code can be made.

On the reservation and in urban Indian enclaves within this country, Indian English augments the informal usage patterns of the speaker's Indian language and in some instances replaces that code. Indian English can be used as the language of the home or the language for daily conversation within the community. It is also the variety of English which many Indian students bring with them when they enter the classroom for the first time.

Specific tabulations on the numbers of persons speaking this English variety have yet to be made. Consistent observations about the nonstandard quality of classroom English added to the more detailed comments on first- and second-language usage patterns within reservation contexts suggest the phenomenon is not localized within a few Indian communities. This statement does not preclude the fact that many Indian English speakers also have control over the conventions of standard English,[3] but they use this style in situations outside the reservation as a diglossic complement to the reservation style.

How long Indian people have been speaking Indian English is subject to debate. Dillard (1972, chap. 4) argues that the pidgin or trade English (from which he traces the development of black

English) also provided the basis for the Indian English code. He suggests further that Indian familiarity with English initially arose from contact with runaway slaves who had control over the pidgin and that this explains why so many white men, in the explorations of the central and western parts of the United States, found Indians who already knew how to speak some variety of English.

Dozier (1970) on the other hand, traces the origins of the code to a more recent influence: the leveling effects of Indian enrollment at Haskell and Carlisle Institutes. Educational policy of that period demanded an English-only school environment. This required non-fluent speakers to develop familiarity in an operational classroom code. Because of the diversity in the students' native language backgrounds, it became the only code which all Indian students had for common use outside the classroom. This lingua franca, he argues, was passed to new Indian students as they entered the boarding school and then spread back to the reservation after graduation.

Indian English may be distinguished from standard English on all levels of its structural detail. The rules of sentence formation which generate acceptable Indian English utterances differ from those required to produce the equivalent utterances in the standard language. Some example sentences, typical of those used by speakers from a New Mexican pueblo community, illustrate the point:

> That man, he be the governor.
> Two womens was out there fighting.
> They are in authority in pertains to actual church functions.
> You have your belief in the corn.
> Each pueblo comes to its own authority.

There is evidence to suggest, however, that the specific details of Indian English structures vary considerably from one Indian community to the next. Analysis has shown that the Indian English code of a given community is a kind of synthesis of English vocabulary and local Indian language grammar and phonology. Thus the Indian English sentences given above are virtually lexical translations from equivalent sentences in the Indian language also controlled by the speech community in question, with the lexical items pronounced as if they were Indian words (Leap 1973a). The only significant divergence from Indian language structure lies within the sentence word order. Equivalent Indian English sentences given by persons from a neighboring speech community where a different Indian language is spoken will agree in their lexical detail with the example sentences above, yet differ in their intonation pattern, their segmental phonology, and their specific morphemic constructions. These differences correlate exactly with the structural features which distinguish the Indian languages of the two communities. Given that there may be as many as 127 different Indian languages still spoken in the United States, there could conceivably be as many as 127 different varieties of Indian English, each with its own phonological and grammatical component. When Indian people admit that they can pinpoint an outsider's tribal origin by "the way he speaks his English," they, too, allude to this possibility.

Indian English, then, is a uniquely Indian way of speaking English since its structural detail mirrors the structure of the Indian language associated with the specific Indian community. Nevertheless, Indian English does have a semblance of pantribal uniformity in that all varieties of the code depart in their structural detail from standard language conventions and frequently do so in similar structural fashions.

The code has pantribal similarity in a second sense: there is evidence to suggest that the local English variety has become the acceptable (and expectable) style of English expression within each community context where it is employed.

This point was made clear to me in recent discussions with students and staff at one of the day schools in the Albuquerque area. The principal (who is Indian but not from the local community) and the Anglo teachers are greatly concerned that many of their pupils speak what the staff regards as a nonstandard variety of English and use that pattern when writing papers or giving oral reports. The Anglo staff members and the principal have resisted efforts to teach the Indian language in the classroom; they feel this would divert student attention from efforts to gain control over the language of privilege—a skill needed for successful completion of high school programs (which will be off the reservation in county school facilities) and for successful entrance into college or the local job market.

The members of the teaching staff from the local Indian community assert that there is nothing wrong with their students' English and add, "if there is a language problem in the school, it lies in the fact that the students do not know how to speak their own Indian language." Hence the teacher aides and Indian teachers take the opposite point of view on language policy and feel that programs to develop Indian language fluency are most necessary within their classroom. I discussed this with several parents, many of whom said they had never noticed any problem with their children's

English. Some added that occasionally they heard what sounded like a Spanish accent but assumed it was due to the number of "Spanish women" who help out at the day school.

This perception of contrast between the English spoken locally and Spanish-American English suggests the extent to which the local English has come to provide a formal linguistic marker of a person's membership within the community life of that particular Indian pueblo. In similar fashion, control over standard English conventions gives formal indication of a person's mobility outside of the pueblo context. For this reason, persons whose business and social activity requires standard language fluency are quick to note the amount of conscious change they must introduce into their English expression when they return to the reservation to guarantee that people will not think they are "putting on airs" by "trying to talk like a white man."

The identification which stems from a community member's control over both the local English and the standard English varieties is worth noting, given our present purpose. Yet the presence of these two English styles within the community raises some additional speculations. For if control over Indian English structure does not preclude control over standard language conventions, then there is no linguistic reason why a specifically Indian English need exist within any segment of the native American population. It might be easy to view these codes simply as responses to the need to maintain Indian identity within a surrounding non-Indian world. Such an explanation would have powerful political implications (indeed, it is the basis of the red English concept, to be discussed below). Yet this conclusion cannot be accepted without first considering some additional language-related factors.

First, some characteristics of English itself need to be considered. All languages yield to the development of special styles for use in special situations; the linguistic structure of English lends itself especially to this kind of variability. Phonologically, for example, while we can set up nine contrastive vocalic segments as part of an overall phonemic pattern, native speakers need employ only six of them to make contrasts in their own local dialect. Part of the development of English fluency involves learning ways to equate phonemic details of another speaker's dialect with the specifics of one's own phonetic inventory.

Grammatically, English surface structure is characterized by a non-reliance on inflectional contrast for meaning discrimination. The specifics of lexical reference and surface level word ordering supply the primary basis for sentence interpretation. This is why a sentence like *Two womens was out there fighting* can be understood in spite of the apparent errors in grammatical agreement.

For these reasons it is quite possible for two people to speak English with quite variant phonological and morphemic structures without these differences inhibiting the message exchange. Indian English—as one such English variety—works as well as any other variety in this regard.

From a cultural point of view intralanguage varieties are never given functional equality. Since any social code always can be identified with the social segment from which it was developed, a given code is deemed appropriate only for use within the purview of that segment. Thus it is frequently deemed desirable to have one style— a so-called standard language—which allows all speakers to express their ideas in an idiosyncratically neutral (or nonsectarian) fashion. Standard language also provides a linguistic means through which a person can overcome the specifics of his social background, because through this medium he can talk on anyone's terms rather than his own.

For English speakers standard language conventions (the use of *shall* instead of *will* in the first person singular future; *you* instead of *you all* as the second person plural pronoun; *is not* instead of *ain't* in the third person singular present, and so on) are not based on linguistic necessity, but have been derived from an extra-linguistic propriety. None of these constraints are essential to the linguistic effectiveness (or grammaticality) of English sentence construction.

Given that standard language conventions are amplifications of speaker competence, control over these conventions can result only from deliberate cultivation. This may be the reason why school authorities place great emphasis on English language training in all schooling programs, especially in situations where the possibility of upward mobility is the most apparent. In school programs where the participants are judged not to be within the cultural mainstream, the problem calls for more specialized attention. A wide variety of teaching materials are now being developed by the public and the private education industry alike with this precise purpose in mind. The pedagogical orientations of these materials fall into one of three general categories: some address themselves to the universal patterns of the child's conceptual development; some employ immediate reinforcement techniques for acquisition of sequenced language skills;

some stress the audio-lingual approach of the pattern drill and sentence repetition. Each program then has its own technique to recommend it. Yet all such programs have one thing in common: given that language learning is a natural process and that standard language conventions augment preexisting knowledge, the programs assume that effective language learning results from effective language teaching—proper introduction to the information the student needs to control. (The programs differ, of course, in the specifics of what this proper introduction should entail.) From the point of view of linguistic theory, this position is perfectly valid. Any student will bring into the classroom the so-called innate familiarity with the constraints of natural language grammar which all human beings, as human beings, are said to possess. What is required, it would therefore seem, is a systematic introduction to the ways these general constraints apply to the process of English sentence formation. Hence the reliance on sequenced drill or situational reinforcement in the programs listed above.

Such a perspective overlooks the important fact that the student, upon entering the classroom, already had put these innate constraints into conversational practice when fluency in his native language or in the Indian English of the community was developed. Thus the student may already be speaking in terms of a localized language standard. Of course these local styles represent the sorts of linguistic expertise that English-as-a-second-language programs are designed to augment, but given the fact of the preexisting fluency, the augmentation cannot come merely through a carefully directed exposure to linguistic alternatives. Some means has to be found to help the student maintain effective control over the language styles which the community context deems appropriate, while developing control over the style the school program now requires him to learn. Effective bilingual speakers achieve such a balance in performance in the real world—the process linguists reify under terms like code-switching or multilingual fluency. But this aspect of the natural language learning process is rarely addressed in the classroom, perhaps because of the unilineal commitment to standard language fluency which all programs (and most of their teachers) inherently possess.

As a result, the student becomes faced with contrastive standards of speaking without receiving encouragement to do what the student would naturally be inclined to do—try to develop control of both structures without sacrificing control over either. Indian English, as a synthesis of native language deep structure and English lexical vocabulary, is the natural result of this learning process. This was certainly the case, as Dozier (1970) points out, for those students who entered the classroom at Haskell and Carlisle without English familiarity. For the student who is already fluent in Indian English the situation is equally serious: the classroom allows him to augment his control over English vocabulary without guaranteeing that the specifics of sentence construction which should accompany that knowledge will also be developed. In essence the school programs enhance fluency over the language style the classroom context is designed to overcome.

There is every reason for people to accept the local English code as the style of speaking appropriate to their own community—it is the style which has been developed within that very community context itself. In recent months the local level acceptance has taken on a new interpretation, with the appearance of the concept of red English within various segments of the native American population. The focus on the uniqueness of the Indian way of speaking English disregards local variation in favor of pantribal Indian English styles, much in the same way as Anglos downplay regional differences when they refer to an American way of speaking English. A convergence of emphasis on a product of the Indian's own historical experience results, which can serve to give common expression to the political struggles of otherwise separate Indian communities. Columnists in several of the Indian rights newsletters now employ the style as a written medium, and speakers at political rallies use it (some say, deliberately) in their presentations. The very existence of the code has become a point of pride among many Indian young people. One Indian's analysis is quite suggestive of the attitude: "See this shows just how far we were willing to go along with the demands to learn the white man's ways, but how we were able to meet those demands on *our* terms."

It is not surprising to find that the acceptance of Indian English occurs simultaneously with the rising stress on native American subject matter in the Indian classroom, and is accompanied by the increasing emphasis on the need to use classroom facilities to further the development of Indian language fluency. All of these concerns are familiar expressions of the heightening self-awareness which always accompanies supracommunity political solidarity. Notice, however, that through this process Indian English becomes the means for developing political awareness, not the focus of political indictment that might otherwise be expected. From the strictly linguistic point of view there is no reason why a community cannot develop fluency in all the language styles for which its members have immediate need, standard language conventions not being any exception. If, therefore, a code exists which purports to have standard language tendencies but which clearly is at variance with standard language structure, we can only conclude that some additional factors have conditioned the deliberate development of the nonstandard code. In that sense, any activity which furthers the continuation of that code, serves the same interests as the factors which conditioned the development of the code to begin with.

If, as might be expected, the existence of Indian English can be traced to the same forces which perpetuate black English and other ethnically based English language styles, then formalized acceptance of the Indian English code, regardless of the semblance of political expediency which may accompany it, furthers the effectiveness of segregation which has long characterized the mainstream's treatment of social minorities—and does so by legitimizing the segregation as part of a more general "self-determination" process. The United States Civil Rights Commission's recent analysis of Indian unemployment problems has made it perfectly clear that the greatest obstacle to Indian economic success is their lack of control over a work-related English. As a result Indian people seeking employment outside of the reservation context enter the job market in unskilled or semi-permanent positions. It is no wonder that the percentage of employed Indian men who hold such jobs is some four hundred times higher than the equivalent percentage for the labor force as a whole (Swanson, 1972).

The idea of a Native American Development Bank, designed to make direct capital allocations available for reservation community self-development, is now being suggested as one way to alleviate this problem. The proposal argues that economic success for Indian people can best be achieved on Indian land, under Indian control (Ewasiuk et al. 1973). No one familiar with the sequence of economic exploitation, which is the history of Indian people in America since the time of contact, can argue against this proposal in theory. Yet the appeal of the proposal must be weighed carefully against the impact the program will have on the two factors which create an Indian unemployment problem to begin with: the local economy does not have a sufficient capital base from which to generate sufficient employment for the indigenous work force; jobs may now exist but the necessary technical skills have not been made available to all segments of the Indian labor force to allow these positions to be filled. Granted the introduction of capital will address itself to the first factor, but this effectively bypasses attention to the second factor. If the student knows that employment can be secured within the reservation context, there need be no demand for local schooling and training programs to provide more adequate control over the kinds of skills necessary for off-reservation employment. NADB would, in fact, lend itself most suitably to a community where educational priorities are oriented toward reservation-defined education and training. The most recent educational directives of the Bureau of Indian Affairs (the CHOICE program detailed in Hawkins 1973) have been designed with precisely this objective in mind. Implementation of this program to decentralize the administration of BIA-related educational activity has already begun, with the ultimate goal of giving each Indian community the option of setting as much of the direction of its local schooling program as community leadership deems appropriate. This means in effect that the priorities in Indian education are now to be determined by Indian people themselves, not by Washington.

No one who examines the history of Indian education policy in this country[4] can deny that for far too long white man's priorities have dominated Indian classroom instruction. In that sense, the CHOICE program seems to offer an alternative to past commitment. But if the community's educational priorities become defined with a policy of on-reservation economic inclusion, are stimulated by the creation of artificial on-reservation employment possibilities, and are accompanied by the acceptance of the community-specific and linguistically artificial Indian English code, we might well wonder whether an alternative to the de facto segregation of previous years has really been achieved.[5]

The present discussion has raised two points which need final reiteration: While it may appear that red English has great utility as a focal point for social and cultural identity, an analysis which treats this code as a logical extension of the national Indian rights struggle is just as guilty of bad science as one which deals with Indian English solely in terms of historical events of three centuries ago, leaving without comment any factors which may have bridged the gap from past formation to present continuation. The existence of Indian English—or any other notion which allows social or cultural identification—cannot be accepted merely on face value. Before reaching such an "objective" conclusion, an analysis must consider most carefully the underlying facts of existence to which the presence of any such concept will inescapably allude.

As a second point: With such an understanding of the full detail of the background comes a special kind of sociocultural perspective. The investigator is in a position to view an assertion of identity in terms of its historical formation as well as its current expediency. Such a perspective reveals the inherent contradiction in the use made of the identity concept. That is, while such a concept purports to supply a symbol for group identification, in reality it reifies the given situation in terms of the conditions which produced the need for the identity concept to begin with, conditions which—as in the instance discussed here—have provided the very means for marking the identification itself. The investigator is free to reach such conclusions; the investigator does not have to live in terms of the contradictions. The kind of objective, nonpartisan science to which many members of our profession trace their identity assumes that such historically based contradictions should not be interfered with and that being outsiders to a given situation somehow exempts them from the responsibilities of social awareness. These observers, like the uncritical advocates of the red English concept, become part of the problem which the struggle now seeks to overcome.

NOTES

1. My thanks to Elizabeth A. Brandt, Grace Holt, Walt Wolfram, John J. Bodine, Nancy Modiano, and M. Estellie Smith for their assistance with details of the present argument. Thanks also to Shirley Hicks for preparing numerous drafts of this manuscript. The analysis of Indian English presented here was developed in conjunction with the Indian Education Project of the Center for Applied Linguistics. It should be noted, however, that the viewpoint expressed in this paper does not necessarily reflect that of the Project nor of the Center.

2. While several comments on Indian, reservation, or dormitory English have appeared within several recent publications (for example, Dillard 1972:139-163; Mitchell and Allen 1967), the comments of Ohannessian (1967:11) on the absence of substantive descriptions of Indian English styles still seem accurate. Steps toward alleviating this deficiency are currently being taken by Barbara Ward, Gina Harvey, and others. Some of the educationl implications of Indian English codes are discussed in Modiano, Leap, and Troike (1973). This author has also discussed the structural details of the Indian English of one pueblo community (Leap 1972; 1973a) and has raised some more general questions concerning the issues in the study of Indian English, building in part on the arguments being presented here (Leap 1973b).

3. As in any instance of standard language conventions, standard English refers to the set of usages which persons in positions of economic, political, and educational power deem appropriate and proper for various conversational contexts. The evaluation implied by the term *standard English* does not necessarily reflect a notion of linguistic adequacy (i.e., nonstandard sentences are just as well formed as standard ones), but it does remind us that a failure to

follow the standard convention in conversational usage may bring about evalua-
tions on the speaker's personal ability, background, and potential which will
extend beyond the person's linguistic skills. As such the standard language of
any group could more accurately be characterized as the language of privilege
(see Lenin 1968).

4. See, for example, the analysis in Liebowitz (1971).

5. One counterargument can be given. There is no reason to demand, as
seems to have been the case up till now, that Indian people seek their personal
fulfillment outside of the home context, or that standard English be the only
linguistic medium to allow this personal fulfillment. Such an argument sets
the self-sufficient reservation as the goal of all social planning. The development
of educational and economic policies in terms of this commitment can be just
as repressive as are the present policies which necessitate off-reservation migration without developing the skills adequate and necessary for off-reservation
adjustment. Both positions implicitly emphasize some possibilities and downplay
the feasibility of others. Both positions treat the individual as a sort of social
pawn. But it is apparent that both alternatives have resulted from the continual
refusal of persons at all levels of authority and power to equate the quality
of achievement with the quantity of promise, and a direct confrontation with
those refusals—and those individuals—seems more in point to this writer.

REFERENCES

Dillard, J. L., 1972. *Black English* (New York: Random House).

Dozier, Edward, 1970. *The Pueblo Indians of North America.* (New York:
Holt, Rinehart and Winston).

Ewasiuk, William J., et al., 1973. Finance and Management: The Key to Indian
Self-determination. (Report prepared for the Bureau of Indian Affairs by
the Department of Agricultural Economics and Economics, Montana State
University.)

Fuchs, Estelle, and Robert Havighurst, 1972. *To Live on This Earth: American
Indian Education* (Garden City, N. Y.: Doubleday).

Hawkins, James, 1972. Recommended Procedures for the Implementation of
CHOICE (Washington: Bureau of Indian Affairs).

Leap, William L., 1972. Subject and Object Agreement in Two Isletan Languages.
(Paper presented at the XII Annual American Indian Language Symposium,
American Anthropological Association, Toronto.)

————, 1973a. Language Pluralism in a Southwestern Pueblo: Some Comments
on Isletan English. In *Bilingualism in the Southeast*, Paul Turner, ed. (Tucson:
University of Arizona Press), pp. 275-293.

————, 1973b. Some Comments on Indian ("Red") English. (Paper presented
at Workshop II, Southwestern Circle of Linguistics, Albuquerque.)

Liebowitz, Arnold, 1971. *Education Policy and Political Acceptance: The Imposition of English as the Language of Instruction in American Schools*
(Washington: ERIC Clearinghouse for Linguistics).

Lenin, Vladimir I., 1968. Critical Remarks on the National Question. In *National
Liberation, Socialism, and Imperialism* by Vladimir I. Lenin (New York:
International Publishers). pp. 13-15.

Mitchell, Emerson Blackgorse, and T. D. Allen, 1967. *Miracle Hill: The Story
of a Navaho Boy* (Norman: University of Oklahoma Press).

Modiano, Nancy; William L. Leap; and Rudolph C. Troike, 1973. *Language
Policy in Indian Education* (Arlington: Center for Applied Linguistics).

Ohannessian, Sirarpi, 1967. *The Study of the Problems of Teaching English
to American Indians: Report and Recommendations* (Arlington: Center for
Applied Linguistics).

Swanson, John, 1972. Press Release on Indian Unemployment. *American Indian
Law Newsletter* 5(17):249-251.

The Emergence of Contemporary Eastern Creek Indian Identity

J. ANTHONY PAREDES

AMERICAN Indians have demonstrated remarkable persistence in maintaining themselves as a social and cultural component of the national life of the United States.[1] Despite centuries of warfare, disease, miscegenation, acculturation, and extreme pressure to assimilate, Native Americans endure. In recent years many individuals and groups on reservations, in cities, and in other areas have received national publicity for dramatic actions which they have taken in their zealous determination to protect their "right to be Indian." Indeed it begins to appear that it is precisely their identity as Indians which is the major asset many American Indians have in seeking means to obtain the greatest benefits of American institutions even though countless thousands of individual Indian descendants have quietly been assimilated into mainstream America.

However, American Indian identity is neither uniform nor static. Particular forms of Indian identity show considerable variability as a result of differences in traditional culture, contact history, degree of acculturation, local conditions, community size, and a host of other variables. Indian identity does not exist in a vacuum, but in the context of perceived contrasts with non-Indians and of a particular view of history. Similarly changes in the forms and evaluation of American Indian identity must be understood in relation to the changing character of the social environment impinging upon Indians and their communities.

The major outlines of the sociocultural effects of historic shifts in national policy toward Indians are well known. Lurie (1971) provides an excellent overview of significant changes in the character of United States Indian adaptations from first contact with whites to the Nixon years. She further notes that in many respects Canadian Indian developments tend to recapitulate those of the United

States as Canadian policy follows patterns similar to those of an earlier period in the United States. In both nations the modern response of a significant portion of Indians may be characterized as an "articulatory movement" which is distinguished from revitalization movements and related phenomena by, among other things, its contractual emphasis in dealing with the larger society in pursuit of the ultimate goal of genuine cultural pluralism (Lurie 1971:418). However conceived, there is nevertheless a current major surge of interest by Native Americans in maintaining their separate identity as Indians while at the same time improving their material conditions in the modern world. Just as Indian survival strategies of the past must be viewed as reactions to the shifting postures of Euro-American governments, modern developments, too, must be understood in the context of the larger sociocultural systems which encompass Indian individuals and communities.

Modern American Indians have a multiplicity of ties to the larger society. The very complexity of contemporary society and Indians' involvement in it present great difficulty in identifying specific features of the larger, total sociocultural system which have been instrumental in shaping the course of development of Indian identity. In this paper data from a small, nonreservation, rural community in Alabama are presented which demonstrate the importance of particular events in shaping the development of one example of contemporary Indian identity. Viewed as a microcosm of Indian identity processes compressed in time and space, this case may have more general implications for understanding current revitalizations of "Indianness."

In the 1970 United States census 2,443 people of Alabama identified themselves as American Indian. Over twenty percent of those who identified themselves as Indians are reported from one county, Escambia. The five to six hundred Escambia County Indians are residentially concentrated in a vicinity called Poarch approximately seven miles northwest of the town of Atmore (population c. 8,000). Although some of these people are physically indistinguishable from whites as a result of intermarriage, the group as a whole is locally regarded by non-Indians as Indian. In addition to Indians at Poarch, there are a number in the town of Atmore itself, families scattered throughout Escambia and surrounding counties, and perhaps several hundred more who originate from Poarch but have emigrated to Mobile, Pensacola, Wisconsin, the Chicago area, and many other places. These people are all descendants of Creek Indians who were not removed to Oklahoma in the 1830s, but managed to remain in their original territory.

Despite the relatively large size of the group and their firmly established local reputation as Indians, very little research has been done heretofore on these eastern Creeks. Frank Speck (1947) visited the group for a few days in 1941 and published a brief report. Gilbert's (1949) brief description of the group is based on Speck's report, and Berry (1963) makes only a passing reference to the group noting that they are one of the few eastern remnant groups with an undisputed tribal pedigree. The absence of earlier research is particularly unfortunate since events of the late nineteenth and early twentieth centuries appear to have been crucial to the formation of the present community and to establishing the background against which developed the contemporary Creeks' revival of interest in their Indian heritage.

For much of their history the eastern Creeks appear to have been generally indifferent to or even rejected their identity as Indians. Their status as Indians was ignored or denied by the federal government until recently; they have received none of the educational, medical, or other benefits available to reservation Indians. Neither have they been legislatively recognized and administered by the state government in contrast to, for example, the Lumbees (Dial and Eliades 1971) and Catawbas (Hudson 1970:73) who historically have been acknowledged officially by the states where they live. Nonetheless, for a variety of reasons including the dark skin color of many, in the past the Escambia County Creeks have been objects of suspicion, prejudice, and discrimination by certain elements of local white society. The Creeks in turn have been careful to maintain social boundaries between themselves and the blacks. In part because of discrimination, many of the Creeks have experienced extreme poverty and a marginal economic existence. For more than one hundred years these Alabama Creeks did little to assert their identity as American Indians.

Since the late 1940s there have been major, if not revolutionary, changes in the eastern Creek Indian community. During the past twenty-five years the Indians of Escambia County have made extraordinary economic and educational gains, and perhaps more importantly they, along with scattered Creek descendants elsewhere in the region, have experienced a generalized revitalization of their social identity as American Indians and as Creeks.

The process of Indian identity formation among the eastern Creeks may be traced through four major stages. Although many of the details of this process are incompletely known at present and may never be recovered for the earliest periods of development, the major stages of the process may be delineated by a series of events regarded as benchmarks in the contemporary Creek view of their own history.

Phase I: From the Creek War to World War I. According to local tradition the ancestors of the Escambia County Creeks were Friendly Creeks during the Creek War of 1812-1814. The founder of the present Poarch community was one of the sons of a Lynn McGhee who is reputed to have been a guide for Andrew Jackson and was rewarded for his services with a tract of land. In the vicinity of Escambia County, common family names of nonremoval Creeks include Gibson, Manac, Colbert, Rolin, as well as McGhee. Some of these families may have been simply backwoods "squatters" in the early days, but Lynn McGhee did receive an allotment of 640 acres, divided into three roughly equal parcels, by special acts of Congress in 1836 and 1837. However, the United States government retained title to the McGhee lands, and it was not until 1924 that a fee simple patent was issued by the government to the heirs of Lynn McGhee. The present-day Poarch community developed around one portion of the McGhee grant land, and another Indian community emerged around a second portion of the land near Huxford, Alabama. (The Huxford Indian community has largely dispersed during the recent past.) Over the years Indians have acquired additional lands through homesteading and purchase. The Indian community did not emerge as a single unit but as a series of distinct hamlets.

Available information is sketchy, but it appears that the Poarch Creeks remained relatively isolated from non-Indians well into the twentieth century. Even social interaction among the several Indian hamlets was generally restricted to special occasions. Atmore did not come into existence until the 1880s, and many older Creeks now living were employed by whites in the early decades of this century clearing the virgin timber, tapping turpentine, and cutting railroad ties for the first railroads through the Poarch area. According to the oldest informants, in the early 1900s the Indians were scattered out in the woods on small patches connected by footpaths, and very few white or Negro families lived in the immediate vicinity. By necessity the Creeks remained largely self-sufficient.

Native speakers of the Muskogee language survived until the end of the nineteenth century (a few individuals living today can recall isolated phrases and words learned from parents and grandparents). A few native traits, such as the making of *sofkee* and use of the word *sofkee*, continued much longer. Social cohesiveness of the Escambia County Indian community in these early days was supported in large part merely by geographic isolation from outsiders. In this phase of Escambia County Creek history as well as the succeeding one, there appears to have been little, if any, formal leadership and political organization. Social ties were primarily those of family, kinship, and locality. Each of the Indian hamlets had a community hall built with communal labor and serving as a recreation center, church, and school. Members of the community and occasional traveling Baptist preachers conducted church services. Schools were operated on a per child fee basis with parents hiring anyone who could be engaged to teach the children to read and write. Many of the Creeks who grew up during this period never really learned to read and write.

Until about the time of World War I, then, although interaction with outsiders was rapidly increasing, the social identity of Poarch Creeks vis-à-vis others appears to have been rather amorphous and of little conscious concern. Nonetheless the specifically Indian identity of the Creeks was maintained by the oral traditions, knowledge of Creek language, and herbal lore of the "older heads." The racial distinctiveness of this older generation was marked and is often expressed today in the form, "old man so-and-so hardly had no moustache—he was a full-blood." More importantly a series of land issues served to make clear the special status of the Poarch people as Indians. Stories had persisted through the years that the Creeks would receive "Indian money" for lands taken from their ancestors. In 1906 many of the Creeks paid a fee to a "lawyer who came through this country" in order to be "written up" for an Eastern Cherokee fund, even though prudent Creeks advised their relatives and friends not to waste their money since they were Creek Indians and not Cherokee. In addition a series of misunderstandings arose over timber rights and the tax status of the McGhee grant land, and some of the acreage was alienated from the Indians. An elderly informant poignantly recalls a visit which he and another Indian made to a lawyer to clarify the status of the land:

> And he said, "I ain't going to tell you what I got to say about it, but what the President got to say." And he got out a big law book and read what was in there to us, "this land granted to old man Lynn McGhee

and his heirs and can't be taxed as long as grass grow and water run."
Well, you know that's a long time. (Slightly paraphrased)

While his recollection may not be entirely accurate, it does embody
the sentiments over land issues which laid the foundations for later
phases in the development of the Escambia County Creeks' sense
of their unique identity.

Phase II: Transition and Discrimination. By the late 1900s the
peasant-like autonomy of the Escambia County Creeks had come to
an end. More and more people were entering wage labor as agricultural and timber workers. Some were beginning "to work on halves"
(sharecropping) for white landholders. The county began requiring
what amounted to corvée labor in maintaining the dirt roads through
the area, and the county school board assumed the responsibility of
paying teachers for the Indian schools. The period from World
War I to about 1948 was a phase in the emerging social identity of
the Escambia County Creeks characterized by rising economic expectations and overt discrimination by whites.

As early as the 1920s some Creek families emigrated to other
parts of the state and to Florida in search of a better life. Many of
those who remained in the Poarch area were moving further
and further afield in seasonal farm work, as timber workers, and
as sharecroppers. However, this was also the period of "the Hoover
years" (the Great Depression) when many families who had begun
to experience a certain amount of affluence as a result of the economic
development of the Atmore area were forced to revert to a near
subsistence level of existence. Immediately following these years
at least one notable Creek individual recovered sufficiently to acquire
a reputation for himself as a modestly successful entrepreneur in
the harvesting of pulpwood. During the 1930s increasing numbers
of Alabama Creeks were periodically migrating to such distant
places as Frostproof, Florida, for agricultural labor. Although it is
difficult to determine exactly when it first occurred, it was probably
toward the end of this period that some of the Creek Indians themselves began "hauling hands" (contracting for and transporting field
hands), eventually going as far as North Carolina and Wisconsin.
During World War II a number of the eastern Creeks served in
the military (some Creeks had seen duty in the Civil War and World
War I), and others became defense workers, primarily at the shipyard
in Mobile.

This was also the period of the marked, formal exclusion of
Escambia County Creeks from white schools. Indian descendants

in surrounding counties were permitted to attend white schools from the earliest days and continued to do so throughout modern history. In Escambia County after the county school board began to pay teachers for the Indians—sometime during World War I or shortly thereafter—these schools became known as Indian schools and operated as a third system in addition to Negro and white schools. (In some cases this procedure may have been partly the result of the Indians' own desires.) These Indian schools were poorly financed and still conducted in the old community halls in each of the Indian hamlets. In one settlement white and Indian schools were only a few hundred yards apart. The county school board consolidated the several Indian schools into a single Consolidated Indian School near the McGhee grant land at Poarch in 1939, but no new building was erected for the school.

After consolidation and to some extent before, Indian children were bussed from miles around (notably from the Huxford area) to the Indian schools, even though a white school might be nearer to their homes. Quite inadvertently, the school board's consolidation of several formerly independent Indian schools served to unify the county's Indian community. Although Indian children were permitted to attend secondary schools in the town of Atmore itself if they could find lodging with friendly town families, public transportation to junior and senior high schools was not provided to Indians; thus very few Indians received more than a rudimentary elementary school education. In addition during this time some Indians were refused service at some businesses and suffered other indignities. Today's Creeks have in mind these dark years when they say that certain whites were "hard on the Indians" and "being Indian was something people tried to hide—seemed like they were ashamed of."

The Poarch Indian community was subject to other forces of change which, while serving to enhance individual self-images, were ultimately socially divisive. In 1929 the Atmore Episcopal priest and a missionary couple began work among the Poarch Indians. Many of the Indians soon converted to the Episcopal faith, three church buildings were erected, catechism classes were conducted, and the Indians received the benefit of a regular clergy. In addition to their spiritual work, the Episcopalians began various programs and efforts to meet the health and educational needs of the Indians. This work has continued to the present through the services of various personnel (cf. Speck 1947:197). At about the same time that the Episcopalians began missionizing, white adherents of the Holiness sect also began preaching to the Indians. Before long the Episcopalians and the Holiness people were in conflict, and many who had originally joined the Episcopal church converted to the Holiness belief. The Holiness Church appears to have served as a personal redemptive movement (Aberle 1966:316) for a significant segment of the Poarch community. Holiness belief continues strongly today, and the largest Indian congregation is a Holiness church pastored by a local Creek Indian. In addition to Episcopal-Holiness competition, in both churches splinter groups have split off over ideological differences. Parallel to the religious segmentation of the community, further discord over the grant land arose within the community in the wake of confusion following the issuance of the fee simple patent for the grant land in 1924.

Despite the social divisions which developed earlier, the end of this second phase of eastern Creek Indian identity development is marked by vigorous actions taken by a core of Creek Indians to improve educational opportunities for their children. Shortly after World War II several outspoken Indians became increasingly impatient with poor discipline at the Indian school, the incompetence of some of the teachers, and the exclusion of Indians from public transportation to secondary schools in Atmore. One parent, one of the few who had received some education in the town of Atmore, informally organized a rather effective boycott of the school. Another stood in the road and blocked the passage of the high-school-bound bus. Yet another, Calvin W. McGhee, with the aid of a young white attorney who had moved to Atmore from another part of the state, initiated a lawsuit against the school board in 1947. In addition McGhee and a delegation of Creek men visited Governor James E. Folsom to present their grievances, and they received a sympathetic hearing. According to some informants the school board attempted to compromise with McGhee, offering to provide bus service to his own and other light-complexioned children but not to the darker ones. McGhee vehemently rejected the offer saying, "My people are all of one family . . . we are all what you would call a Creek nation . . . there are many different families which are all Creek and all some way or another run back into the line with the others."[2] The court case apparently was never completed since the school board soon reconsidered its position rather than become embroiled in a complicated and hopeless controversy, not only with the Indians, but also the state and federal authorities. By 1950 the school board had built a modern school building near the old Consolidated Indian School, replaced some of the teachers with better qualified ones, and began providing bus service for the Indian children into the Atmore schools. The stigma of being Indian had begun to be removed; the next step was the transformation of Indian identity into a social asset. The opportunity soon came, ushering in the third and most critical phase of contemporary eastern Creek identity development.

Phase III: Land Claims and Powwows. One of the newly hired teachers at the Poarch school learned by chance of the creation of the United States Indian Claims Commission. She brought this information to men who had been leaders in the school case—particularly Calvin McGhee. Through the teacher and the lawyer who had handled the school suit, Calvin McGhee and his followers obtained the services of a series of attorneys, including one from a neighboring county who had worked for a United States senator at the time the Indian Claims Commission legislation was passed and another attorney who had already worked with the Choctaw Indians of Mississippi on their land claim. Decades of talk of the Indian money and land had set the stage for local enthusiasm for pressing the land claim. Calvin McGhee had demonstrated his leadership abilities in the school issue, and although there were some skeptics, his call for action on the land claim rallied broad support in the Indian community. On October 19, 1950, Creeks from Poarch and surrounding areas held a mass meeting. On advice of their legal advisors, they officially organized themselves as a band of Indians, elected a twelve-member council representing not only the local community but Creek descendants throughout the area, and elected Calvin McGhee as permanent chairman. The group was originally organized as the Perdido Band of Friendly Creek Indians of Alabama and Northwest Florida (the Perdido Creek is an important local landmark); according to one of the attorneys, Calvin McGhee insisted on the term *friendly* because of "certain family traditions" (cf. Hudson 1970: 105-122). Later, as a legal strategy, the name was changed to The Creek Nation East of the Mississippi.

The early days of the land claims activity generated great excitement among Indians and the local populace in general. Considerable publicity began to be given the eastern Creeks and their land claim in newspapers from Mobile, Birmingham, and Pensacola. Thousands of individuals came from a wide area of the Southeast to "sign up for the Indian money" during the 1950s and into the 1960s. Many

people from the immediate vicinity who had never before acknowledged any Indian ancestry came foward to be enrolled, albeit sometimes secretly. As the local joke has it, "there used to be three races
of people around here: White, Indian, and Colored; now there's
only two: Indian and Colored." Suddenly being Indian was a personal asset. Many people were now "proud to claim their Indian."

McGhee led a relentless drive to win the claim. He and other
Indians personally made many trips to Washington supported by
small donations from the local community and from registration
fees. McGhee soon became known as "the Chief," and he became
engrossed in the study of Creek Indian history and the ancestry of
"his people." Chief McGhee emerged as both a powerful charismatic
leader and an extremely effective publicist for the eastern Creeks.
Through his tireless leadership, the Creek Nation East of the Mississippi together with the Oklahoma Creeks finally won a judgment
of several million dollars in 1962, but not until 1972, after McGhee's
death, was the money finally dispersed to the Creek Indians. The
significance of the land claim to the self-esteem of the Escambia
County Creeks is concisely and poetically stated by one informant:
"Even if we [didn't] get one cent of it, I'll always say it was that
Indian money which freed us from bondage . . . because so many of
those who had been so down on the Indians had to face up to us over
that money."

By at least the 1950s McGhee had come to a much broader
vision of his mission. Although the land claim remained the central
focus of his activities, McGhee went far beyond this issue in efforts
to help his people. Through his land claims research he had acquired
a deeper understanding of the history of the Creeks. He established
and nurtured contacts with other eastern Creek descendants, Oklahoma Creeks, and Indians across the nation. Calvin McGhee was
in the delegation which presented the resolutions of the 1961 American
Indian Chicago Conference to President John F. Kennedy. Shortly
before 1960, Chief McGhee began wearing a generalized Plains
Indian costume of his own design at public appearances. With the
assistance of Indian hobbyists who had come to know the Creeks
through the land claim publicity, McGhee and some of the young
men of the community organized an Indian dance team. The Chief
in costume, the dancers (mainly youngsters), and the medicine man
(an elderly Poarch Creek herbalist) attracted much attention to
themselves and to the Creek cause when they appeared at powwows
and various white-sponsored festivals in the area. At about this same

time McGhee organized a political party for Indian descendants in several Alabama counties. Political rallies for candidates for local and state offices were frequently conducted at the Poarch school, and several candidates and politicians at both county and state levels sought Chief McGhee's endorsement and support. While these activities served to strengthen the Indian identity of many of McGhee's followers and certainly brought much publicity to Alabama Indians, some members of the Indian community had serious misgivings. In particular the feathers and powwows were regarded by some with suspicion and were branded as sinful by some of the Holiness people. The issue of powwows and other Pan-Indian activities continues to separate some Holiness adherents from organized activities of the Council of the Creek Nation East of the Mississippi. This division may reflect an underlying conflict between two simultaneous and related but very different social movements among the Escambia County Creeks: one of a sacred type grounded in fundamentalist Christianity and the other of a secular form based in part on popular stereotypes of the American Indian. The latter-day dissent of some of the Poarch Creeks notwithstanding, Calvin McGhee did provide effective, unifying leadership in dealing with the two issues on which there was virtually universal consensus: education and the Indian money.

Phase IV: Death of a Leader and New Directions. The rather sudden death of Chief McGhee in 1970 occasioned important new developments which characterize the fourth and current phase of eastern Creek identity formation. Whatever misgivings some of his people may have had about some of his later activities, Chief McGhee's memory became imbued with an almost mystical aura, and he was elevated to the status of a true culture hero by diverse and sometimes competing elements of the Indian community. As some now say, "It wasn't just the Indian money Chief Calvin was after . . . some of these people didn't realize what all he was trying to do for them until it was too late . . . he was trying to bring this tribe back together again . . . bring back the Indian as a race—as a person." McGhee is often credited by his people with having improved the lot of the Indians educationally, socially, and economically, even at the expense of his own financial well-being. It should be noted that it was precisely during the years in which McGhee was most active that the region as a whole was experiencing rapid economic growth and fundamental changes in the overall character of intergroup relations. However it must also be conceded that although the Negro civil rights movement may have been as much benefit to southern Indians as to blacks (Peterson 1971:123), McGhee's direct attack on discrimination against Creek Indians in 1947 antedates the civil rights movement by nearly a decade.

The loss of a forceful, charismatic leader such as McGhee left a gap which was difficult to fill. Nonetheless the transition of leadership within the Council of the Creek Nation East of the Mississippi appears to have been smooth. Shortly before his death Calvin McGhee had requested that one of his sons, Houston, become his successor, and the council agreed. So there was no immediate problem of succession, and Houston quickly assumed his official duties as chairman of the council and spokesman for the Creeks. The chairman-chief remains the central unifying force of the council, but a somewhat wider distribution of responsibility and influence within the council has taken place since the death of Chief Calvin. This has been particularly true since some of the younger people were added to the council in recent years. These younger people have all received at least some high school education, had extensive experience in the outside world, and reached their maturity during the midst of the most intensive land claims activity. Furthermore as a result of Calvin McGhee's accomplishments in popularizing Indianness, after McGhee's death an Indian descendant in an adjoining county organized his own council and claimed chieftancy over all the Creeks east of the Mississippi bolstering his legitimacy through his friendship and claims of kinship with a prominent Oklahoma Creek leader.

During 1971 and 1972 the presence of another contender for the chieftancy served as an important counterpoint against which Houston McGhee and the Poarch-based council played their organizational activity and publicity. A competing eastern Creek organization has been particularly annoying to the Poarch Creeks since theirs is the only concentrated community of Creeks; only they have experienced systematic discrimination, and it was their people who initiated and pursued the land claims case. Even so, beginning with Calvin McGhee and continuing into the present, some Poarch Creek leaders have had a keen interest in building an effective Indian organization which extends beyond the local community and incorporates the thousands of Indian descendants scattered elsewhere. In February 1973, a meeting of the Poarch-based council with representatives of Creeks from other areas in Alabama, Georgia, and Florida was held at Poarch School, and the ascendancy of Chief Houston McGhee and the

Council of the Creek Nation East of the Mississippi was publicly and congenially acknowledged by the contending organization. The issue of which organization legitimately represents the eastern Creeks is potentially of some importance.

Beginning in 1971 the Poarch-based council began negotiating with the state and other agencies for land and funds for an Indian cultural center and recreational complex to be constructed on a nearby interstate highway. The council regards the cultural center as a means for supporting and promulgating Indian identity, as a kind of memorial to Chief Calvin McGhee, as a source of employment for Indians, and as a tourist attraction for the general economic benefit of the Atmore area. In part to support their efforts to develop the cultural center and to receive government recognition as the legitimate representatives of all eastern Creeks, in 1971 the council incorporated as the Creek Nation East of the Mississippi; the council is technically the board of directors. Some white leaders in Atmore are becoming increasingly interested in the economic potential of a cultural center and half jokingly talk about the possibility of an Indian Disneyland. The Indian council is open to advice and assistance from Atmore businessmen, but some of the councilmen evidence concern over the possibility of the project slipping from Indian control.

In addition to Atmore businessmen the Poarch community has received considerable interest from non-Indians in forms that have tended to bolster confidence in the importance of the Indians, their recent history and culture, and what they are undertaking. For example an advertising man who came into contact with the group through an advertising campaign for a product with an Indian motif has recently relocated to Atmore and informally works in behalf of the Indians. Similarly an Indian historian and folklorist from a nearby city has established a friendship with one of the younger council members who is the current director of the Indian dance team, and this scholar advises his Creek friend on matters of Indian history and traditional culture. In this connection, the investigator's own role should not be discounted since the mere fact of his studying "our history and ways" imbues these things with value and dignity from the Poarch Creek point of view.

In 1971 the council instituted an Annual Thanksgiving Homecoming Powwow. The powwow as yet has not attracted many Indians from elsewhere, but has proved highly successful as entertainment and a source of pride to the Escambia County Creeks, and it draws large crowds of white spectators. These activities, as well as the cultural center plans, may have been stimulated to some extent by the termination of classes at the Poarch School in 1969 which came about in part because of various rulings of the Supreme Court. Members of the council recently have participated in planning conferences with non-reservation Indians from throughout the eastern United States. There is a growing interest in reviving elements of traditional Creek culture as well as maintaining Pan-Indian traits. A few young men are openly but not militantly beginning to use the expression *Indian movement* to describe the work of Calvin McGhee, his faithful assistants through the years, and the present leadership. The Indian movement clearly has entered a very complex, fast-paced, and vibrant era, and it is difficult to predict the specific developments of the months and years ahead. Whatever lies ahead, however, the Creek Indians of Escambia County, Alabama, have emerged from obscurity and powerlessness to a position of outspoken pride in their identity as Indians. Although a sizable portion of the Poarch community has not entered fully into these latest stages of the Indian movement and have been content with simply the elimination of overt discrimination, the movement has positively asserted the importance of being Indian in south Alabama.

In brief outline, during the nineteenth century the eastern Creek community began to crystallize relatively undisturbed by outside influences. Beginning near the turn of the century rapid white expansion in their area and economic growth exposed the Escambia County Creeks to major forces of change. Through most of the first half of the century these Creeks were subject to poverty, discrimination, and denigration of their Indian identity. Following World War II events in the Indian community erased much of the stigma of being Indian. And since the 1950s, a series of related developments involving land claims and Pan-Indian activities have led to a full-blown Indian movement involving Indian descendants from throughout the area including the Poarch Creeks. The Indian movement has brought public recognition to the eastern Creeks, and they now seem to have established their identity firmly and positively as American Indians, both socially and personally.

From this brief narrative of the emergence of contemporary eastern Creek Indian identity it can be seen that the process conforms to the general model of revitalization movements (Wallace 1970: 188-99), and the various factors which have been proposed as causes of social movements are all present. Following the evolution of a post-removal, peasant-like eastern Creek folk culture and the achievement of relative homeostasis, there is a period of increasing stress exhibiting the several types of relative deprivation described by Aberle (1966:326-329) and a measure of social disorganization within the community. Next appears the charismatic leader in the person of Calvin McGhee. Since the leader's death he has tended to become enshrined. And there are on-going processes of routinization and accommodation within the current collective leadership of the Indian movement. A detailed analysis of eastern Creek identity formation in terms of revitalization and social movement theory is beyond the scope of this present paper. The following brief discussion merely indicates two features of Indian identity formation processes as they occurred among eastern Creeks which may tend to be slighted in attempts to understand current reassertions of Indian identity. The first has to do with the critical importance of specific historical events. The second and closely related point concerns the role of particular individual outsiders.

In the case of the Escambia County Creeks it is possible to identify rather precisely events in the larger social system without which the course of social revitalization would not have occurred as it did. Some of the events are of a negative character against which the Indian community reacted, most importantly the decisions and actions of the school board to exclude Indians from white schools. Other events were of a positive and supportive character, principally the creation of the United States Indian Claims Commission and the chance learning of its existence by the Poarch Creeks. Critics may deride and dismiss land claims Indianness as synthetic, transient, and spurious, but in this case the land claim provided both the vehicle for broadening social support for the Poarch community and the springboard from which a more general Indian movement developed. It is suggested here that blunt economic motivations for asserting Indian identity should be given more serious consideration. Given the special governmental status of reservation Indians and the romantic thirst of the American public for things Indian, an identity as Indian ultimately may be the most important economic asset held by poorer, smaller Indian communities.

The rather short time span, small community size, and discreteness of eastern Creek Indian identity development enable the analyst to identify quite precisely critical roles played by particular outsiders in the identity formation process. Among these individuals are the missionaries who came to the Indians in the 1920s, Governor Folsom who sympathetically heard the Indians' complaints over education, the young lawyer who assisted in the school case, the school teacher who learned of the Indian Claims Commission, the several attorneys who worked on the land claims—personal pecuniary motives notwithstanding—and in more recent years, a variety of interested outsiders including the investigator himself. During the last two phases of eastern Creek development, the success of the movement has also depended upon the Creeks having sufficient economic resources, collectively and individually, to support the progress of the land claims, the performance of Indian dances, and the cultural center. In large part these resources have been available because of the willingness of outsiders to employ Indians in more profitable occupations since World War II.

Related to the instrumental roles of individual outsiders is the matter of general recognition and sympathetic publicity which the eastern Creeks have received from politicians, the press, and television. Wallace (1970:195) has observed that in complex societies a revitalization movement can effect cultural transformation only if the movement is able to "capture . . . functionally crucial apparatus (such as power and communications networks, water supply, transport systems, and military establishment)." Obviously the Creek movement was not aimed at the transformation of the total society, so these conditions do not really apply. However, even for a movement aimed at a tiny segment of a complex society, at the very least capturing the attention of communications media is extremely advantageous, if not necessary, for success. For as Goodenough has observed in a slightly different context:

> To regard community development as a process of collective identity change, in which a community's members come to look upon themselves as a different kind of people and on their community as a different kind of place, calls attention to the importance of recognition by others—in this case by outsiders. As development progresses, the community's members are eager for words of praise and approval from outsiders, especially those outsiders who have been their severest critics. Such comment reassures them that their efforts are being recognized by others and that they are on the way to a collective identity of which they can be proud within the larger world community. Acquisition of each new symbol of the identity to which they aspire is a noteworthy event. They want everyone to know it and proudly put it on display. (1963:241)

The publicity which the people of the Creek Nation East of the Mississippi have received for their land claims case and, more recently, their powwows and other accomplishments have served them well in their quest for a new identity.

In general, anthropologists may not have examined fully the significance of recent historic events, support from sympathetic outsiders, media publicity, and public recognition as instrumental in current revitalization processes among Native Americans. For it has been in the context of such events and supports that the Indians' own impressive efforts have resulted in the psychological, social, and cultural rebirth of "a forgotten people":[3] the Eastern Creeks.[4]

NOTES

1. The research upon which this paper is based was supported by the Indian Oral History Program, Florida State Museum, University of Florida, Gainesville, Florida, and a Florida State University Council on Faculty Research Support summer grant. Fieldwork was conducted intermittently from December 1971 to May 1972, for three months during the summer of 1972, and continues irregularly to the present. In addition to participant observation and interviewing, the investigator was permitted to examine copies of a number of historical documents in the possession of the people themselves.

I wish to express my appreciation to the many individuals of Atmore who have extended their friendship and help to me and to the Episcopal Diocese of the Central Gulf Coast for providing me with lodging during my summer research. My most heartfelt thanks are extended to the Council of the Creek Nation East of the Mississippi and all the Creek Indian people I have met for their great friendship and hospitality and the cooperative spirit with which they have received my research.

2. The quotation is attributed to McGhee by an informant.

3. The phrase is used by some Eastern Creek leaders themselves to characterize their group.

4. I would like to introduce "Eastern Creeks" as the standard proper noun designation for these people in the anthropological literature rather than the more cumbersome "Creek Nation East of the Mississippi" or the shortened form "Creek Nation—East."

REFERENCES

Aberle, David F., 1966. *The Peyote Religion Among the Navaho*, Viking Fund Publications in Anthropology, No. 42 (New York).

Berry, Brewton, 1963. *Almost White* (New York: Macmillan).

Dial, Adolph, and David K. Eliades, 1971. The Lumbee Indians of North Carolina and Pembroke State University. *The Indian Historian* 4(4):20-24.

Gilbert, William H. Jr., 1949. Surviving Indian Groups of the Eastern United States. In *Smithsonian Report for 1948* (Washington, D. C.: U.S. Government Printing Office), pp. 407-438.

Goodenough, Ward Hunt, 1963. *Cooperation in Change* (New York: Russell Sage Foundation).

Hudson, Charles M., 1970. *The Catawba Nation*. University of Georgia Monographs, No. 18 (Athens, Georgia).

Lurie, Nancy Oestreich, 1971. The Contemporary American Indian Scene. In *North American Indians in Historical Perspective*, Eleanor Burke Leacock and Nancy Oestreich Lurie, eds. (New York: Random House), pp. 418-480.

Peterson, John H. Jr., 1971. The Indian in the Old South. In *Red, White, and Black: Symposium on Indians in the Old South*, Charles M. Hudson, ed. Southern Anthropological Society Proceedings, No. 5, (Athens, Georgia), pp. 116-133.
Speck, Frank G., 1947. Notes on Social and Economic Conditions Among the Creek Indians of Alabama in 1941. *América Indígena* 7:194-198.
Wallace, Anthony F. C., 1970. *Culture and Personality* (New York: Random House).

Portuguese Enclaves:
The Invisible Minority

M. ESTELLIE SMITH

THE growing anthropological emphasis on complex societies has led us to redefine, invent, or place increasing emphasis upon certain concepts and approaches which hold special significance in the study of large-scale, heterogeneous sociocultures.[1] Terms such as *identity*, *boundary*, and *social networks* present us with constructs very different from those usually in the fore when studying tribal society. The latter groups are usually treated (albeit artificially at times!) as isolated units with homogeneous cultures. The cultural variability of complex societies forces us to give up this more simplistic approach, to concentrate more on process than on structure.

The study of various Portuguese-American communities[2] has not only provided some much-needed ethnographic data on these relatively unknown people but also offers interesting insights which are relevant to the above-mentioned methodological concerns. This paper will present the identity profile which emerged after investigations with both insiders (i.e., community members) and outsiders; will offer a historically based explanation for both the peculiarly self-pejorative nature of that profile, as well as the fact that the identity is said to be due to the highly traditional nature of Portuguese-American culture; and finally will discuss the larger, theoretical implications of the data. The diachronic focus of the analysis will stress a processual interplay among sociocultural segments and across the boundaries established by the delineation of Portuguese identity.

An initial methodological problem is the statement of definitions. The terms *identity* and *boundary* have a variety of parameters in the anthropological and sociological literature. As used here *identity* will refer to the characteristics—the modal personality, if you will—which a group generally is said to possess. The resultant profile may

be determined by members of the group in question or may be compared with the identity as perceived by outsiders or by the investigator.[3] Any group possesses a number of identities, and the scientific
observer does well to bear this caveat in mind. The identity elements
of the profile rarely are, nor need they be, consistent. Contradictions
and paradoxes may have positive adaptive value since they allow
an individual to select the appropriate support for behavior—regardless
of which way it goes. This approach to the concept of identity is
much more limited than, say, Barth's who appears to conceive of
the term as having much the same referents as the word *culture*.[4]

Another term of special significance, *boundary*, has markers which
are both real (based on territorial criteria) and abstract (focusing
on social relations and the organization of behavior). Though the
latter boundary is the more important of the two for the social
scientist, it is signficant for this study that only the Portuguese of
London, England, do not live in a territorial enclave—i.e., a spatially
cohesive neighborhood.

In five of the six towns or cities with which I am familiar[5] the
consensus was that physical and social boundaries between the Portuguese and non-Portuguese are clearly drawn. There are of course
networks which cross the boundaries: The Portuguese and non-
Portuguese mix in school, on the job, in sports, and (minimally)
residentially. But in one Portuguese community twenty-three informants were questioned as to whom they would list as their five closest
friends, and nineteen listed no non-Portuguese while the remaining
four listed their three best friends as Portguese. Although the Portuguese do marry out (marriage to a non-Portuguese does not bring
the stranger into the community unless he or she puts forth a concentrated effort to show a preference to affiliate with the Portuguese
rather than his or her natal group), the primary, almost the sole
point of articulation between the Portuguese and non-Portuguese
is in the economic sphere. Members of both groups perceive this lack
of articulation and account for it in terms of Portuguese traditionalism
—that is, a reluctance on the part of immigrants and their descendants
to give up European patterns and accept an American life style.
Some Portuguese argue that they try to be Americans but that various
forces work against it: "I don't want to hurt the old people too
much." "You keep falling back into the old ways because you have
to mix with the Greenies [new immigrants] who come in." "You
work and live with Portuguese all the time and a lot of them don't
want to change." "I don't like a lot of the old ways but my [hus-

band, wife, father . . .] can't seem to break away." But all agree the Portuguese cling to tradition.

Given this apparent emphasis by Portuguese-Americans on the preservation of the parent socioculture, one would not be surprised to find either a positive weighting on their traditional beliefs, values, and social structure or a negative weighting on elements perceived as American. But field data indicate that the reverse is actually the case. This is reflected both in conversations and actual observed behavior. Older women want to Americanize their houses, their cooking, their dress, their life style generally; adult males admire men who don't "behave like Greenies"; and young people consistently remark that a major cause of conflict with parents is the fact that the children are "too American for the parents' liking." Contrariwise, people who are disliked or who are for some reason the object of ridicule are called "dumb Portygees"—with the emphasis on "Portygee" (a highly derogatory term) rather than "dumb." Typical pejorative remarks are: "What do you expect from a Portuguese?" "That's a typical Portuguese for you!" or self-deprecatingly, "That's a Portuguese way of doing it."

Three profiles were obtained: the view which the Portuguese held of themselves; the view which they believed outsiders held of them; the view which outsiders did hold of the Portuguese. There was almost total congruency among the three lists. Since my original study was not aimed at obtaining this information (I was actually concerned only with immigration patterns), my data are not in a form amenable to quantification. Briefly, however, "a typical Portuguese" is hardworking, clean, not too bright, easygoing, respectful of authority, nonambitious, thrifty, oversexed, careful of property, uninventive, unimaginative, hospitable, cheerful, unable to deal with difficult problems or intricate mechanical items, cooperative, passive, and not much trouble to anyone. He is seen as disinterested in community affairs and incapable of organizing for effective political or economic change. A woman is a drudge; hardworking, submissive, and essentially concerned with her home and her family. A number of Portuguese men categorized women as gossipy and always fighting among themselves—causing trouble for men who would be friends with each other were it not for the feuds of the womenfolk. A Fall River Board of Education official claims that the Portuguese are the main reason why that city's educational level is one of the lowest in the nation (8.8 years as compared to approximately 11.0 nationally, and 12.2 for the state).

An analysis of sources—dating from the eighteenth century to the present and ranging from ships' logs, diaries, and novels to scholarly studies and newspaper accounts—reveals that the stereotypic tags used to characterize "the typical Portuguese" not only had an early genesis but remained consistent through time. In the course of examining such material an explanation began to take shape for both the genesis of the profile, particularly its denigrative elements, and its continued persistence to the present time.

United States census data show that some eighty percent of all North American Portuguese immigrants come from the Azores, a group of islands in the mid-Atlantic some nine hundred to twelve hundred miles west of the mainland of Europe. The islands were uninhabited until they were settled by the Portuguese in about 1450. Marginal to continental life the Azoreans lived an impoverished existence and appeared to occupy the position vis-à-vis the motherland of a forgotten stepchild. What wealth was available came from fishing trips to such areas in the New World as Newfoundland's Grand Banks and Georges Banks off Cape Cod. Fishing trips, the great whaling industry which began in the eighteenth century, and the florescence of the maritime mercantilism which reached its height in the nineteenth century, all combined to draw the Azoreans into contact with the outside world—particularly New England. The Azores became known to New Englanders as "the Western Islands Whaling Grounds" and served as a place not only to hunt the highly profitable sperm whales but also to take on fresh supplies of water and food. Azoreans replaced seamen who were either unsuitable or who managed to escape ashore. An 1842 narrative from a ship's log gives some indication of the importance of islanders in the crew's composition: "As the ship put out . . . the crew consisted of four Azoreans, two Irishmen, and eight Americans. At Fayal, one of the nine Azores, eight new crew members were added, five of whom were Azoreans. The other three were Americans waiting in port for a whaling ship in need of additional crew members" (J. Ross Brown, diary, 1842, from Klewin, 1973:69). By 1880 "the ratio of Azoreans in the whaling crews was even greater. . . . A master harpooner . . . noted in his diary that 'all of my crew . . . are Azorean, except one' " (Klewin 1973:69).

The Azorean dorymen joining the Portuguese fleet to fish the North American waters often sailed to New England ports and dumped their fish for sale on American wharfs. Then instead of returning home to their families in the islands, they would fish out of New England. Some men would leave the boats and sail with an American master. Portuguese boats were in the habit of dropping some men who wished to stay and replacing them with men who were homesick for their parents, wives, children, and familiar surroundings. Most of this movement in and out of New England by the Azoreans went unrecorded in the government records and must be surmised from old documents such as ships' logs, marriage records, and the like. A common pattern was to emigrate to the United States to earn the money needed to return home in a few years and buy enough farm land and a good enough boat so that the family's prosperity would be assured.

The Portuguese of the Azores, therefore, unlike the majority of European immigrants from the continent, had a long and intimate contact with Americans and America. Indeed the connections were of greater intensity and immediacy than those with the Portuguese mainland. Further the connection was one of migratory fluidity; an Azorean did not see "a trip to New England for a few years" in the same fashion as continental immigrants saw their permanent departure from their ancestral homes.

This interdigital relationship continued even after the decline of the maritime focus in New England. The textile industry began to boom and demanded labor. Many of the Portuguese came to work in the mills but, again, would return to the islands if a fishing vessel brought news of sickness, a wedding, or other family business. Though an increasing number made the same residential commitment in the United States as non-Portuguese immigrants, the Portuguese always maintained closer ties with those left behind. As late as the 1920s, when most Azoreans were employed in the textile mills, emigration from the United States to the Azores remained remarkably high. From 1900 to 1920 United States census figures show that approximately twenty-five percent of the islanders returned home (the figure probably should be much higher according to informants). Of those who returned, some ninety-four percent remained in the United States less than ten years (Taft 1923:117).

To summarize: The sociohistorical evidence indicates that the Azoreans have been strongly dependent upon the United States since the late eighteenth century. They relied heavily upon the economic edge provided to emigrants by the maritime and milling industries of New England. Yet the marginal existence of island life ill equipped Azoreans for the contacts which they had with New

England. Granted they had a far more realistic view of life in the
United States than did most immigrants, this was more than offset
by their lack of education[6] (so that qualifications set by non-Portuguese employers forced them into the most menial positions) and the
absence of an incentive to carve a place for themselves in the larger
social structure. Other immigrant groups came to New England,
worked at jobs of drudgery for a time, and then employed a number
of techniques to remove themselves from the ranks of the disad-
vantaged immigrant. The Portuguese remained in menial positions,
paying little attention to labor agitators and social reformers alike.
A hard life and unbelievable poverty even by European standards
was their lot whether in the islands, as seamen, or as laborers in
the mills. They were willing to work extremely long hours at
dangerous work for starvation wages, often with a good-natured
smile and at worst with an air of passive resignation. One observer
summed it up when he said, "They are seekers of work, and if
properly handled and guided are as good workers as are to be had
anywhere" (Bannick 1917:60). They were, sociologically, "the niggers
of New England."

Migratory mobility, easy access to news of home, greater ability
to return home for short visits, a nostalgia and sentimentality for
island life, and a constant influx of short-term workers—who moved
back and forth with the nonchalance of a commuter catching the
7:15 to the city—all combined to create the Portuguese-American
identity. Not only did the immigrant from the Azores take a passive
stance regarding the need—so sharply perceived by other foreign
groups—to achieve a place in the power structure (which is not the
same as acquiring the material culture and worldly attitudes of the
socially elite), he also remained sufficiently involved with still later
arriving Greenies to be tagged "traditional." There was none of the
frantic push to learn the essential skills of survival in a strange land;
there was little of the desperate fight to be accepted into the dominant
social system because the die had been cast and it was economically
impossible to return home; there was little of the culture shock
that stems from ignorance and accentuates differences. Thus while
marked cultural change did occur in the base-line patterns of the
Azoreans, they were not in the style which marked the assimilation
of other ethnic groups. The mechanics of the melting pot process
were altered, and the folk response to this was that the Portuguese
were loathe to give up old country ways.

Is it this charge of reluctance to Americanize, however, which accounts for the domination of pejorative elements in the identity profile of Portuguese-Americans? Why do the denigrative elements of slow-wittedness, lack of ambition, unimaginativeness, an unwillingness to learn new things appear to be most significant attributes of the identity profile for the Portuguese from both the insiders' and outsiders' views?

Again the history of the United States-Azorean contact provide at least a partial explanation. As we have seen, the initial contacts between the two groups were based on maritime interests of both the Yankee seafarer and Azorean fisherman. From the descriptions of life in the islands, Azoreans were astonishingly poverty-stricken. The New England sailors and sea captains, on the other hand, were fighting for maritime supremacy and for the riches that this would bring. They were willing to take chances, to innovate, to capitalize on the much-touted Yankee shrewdness and Yankee ingenuity. Psychocultural factors selected out from the maritime trades the more conservative New Englander who kept his feet planted on the farm or his eyes focused on the ledger. As a result, the American seafarers who had the most contact with the Portuguese peasants held a world view much different from the latter's. The impoverished Azorean, like the poor everywhere, was reluctant to try the new and gamble with his small margin of security. Discussions which explain peasant behavior by emphasizing their love of the land, their stolid, unimaginative attitudes, and their innate conservatism, would do better, I think, to emphasize the restrictive parameters within which they operate—the narrow range of choices which the poor see as determining survival or starvation.

The Yankees tried to bring the Azorean into their sphere. "Manifest destiny," "the sky's the limit," "luck-and-pluck/do-and-dare" were the Yankees' slogans and they grew impatient and scornful of these men who would not try new techniques of whaling, invest part of their earnings in a cargo of teas and silks, rum and slaves, or build skimming clippers rather than plodding dorymen. But for the Portuguese a new tool or technique with which one was clumsy might mean death at sea. There was no spare money for a risky investment in a cargo that might never reach port—even if *he* did— and still less money among the islanders to build sailing vessels.

So the Portuguese established a reputation for dullness, a reluctance to change, slowness in learning, and shortsightedness albeit hardworking, brave, and willing to face hardships cheerfully. The Yankee-derived identity was established for a hundred years or more before the shift in occupation and immigration patterns occurred as a result of the movement into the textile mills. And there was nothing, really, in this shift which caused the Yankees to change their minds. Instead of seeing their jobs as the first step in a progression to becoming an entrepreneur and then a captain of industry[7] in the Horatio Alger tradition of the times, the Portuguese for the most part remained laborers—when they did not leave the factory to buy a boat, a small farm, or return home to the islands.

As for the islanders themselves, they were willing to accept this assessment of their identity. It differed little from the profile perceived by the continental Portuguese of these marginal frontiersmen in a poor corner of the Portuguese empire. Further what did it matter what outsiders thought of the Portuguese? Outsiders valued them as workers and that meant jobs and that was the important thing. That Azoreans had little if any entry into the decision-making circles of the power elite, that they had no voice in political or economic affairs was of little concern. When one compared the economic security which resulted from the American connection with life in the islands for those who did not have such a connection, it was of negligible significance that they were excluded from many social spheres in the United States. Did the Yankees, the Irish, the Italians bypass them? How was this different from the way in which they were treated by the Portuguese from the Continent? Such treatment, they reasoned, was the fate of an islander. There was then little resentment or hostility, few attempts to break down and change the situation in the way in which other immigrants fought to become part of the decision-making structure.

Finally the Portuguese could see how the more militant Irish and Italians were discriminated against. "No Irish need apply." "No Micks, Dagos, or Dogs allowed in this Establishment!" Invisibility was protection against such discrimination—especially in relation to employment. Patronizing though the Yankee stereotype might be, it was better than active hostility which often erupted into gang warfare, the burning of houses and even whole blocks which housed an unwanted ethnic group, or the desecration of churches. The Portuguese Sambo stance[8] was good protective coloring.[9]

In summary then the historical period of minimal contact between Yankees and Portuguese established the Yankee view of the Portuguese; gave the Portuguese realistic information concerning life in America which made the initial period of settlement for immigrants less trying; encouraged the Azorean to create regular channels by which he could return home so that an individual who did find the situation in New England intolerable could choose flight rather than a fight; gave foreknowledge of prejudicial attitudes and the "smart way" to get along.

Preliminary data indicate that the Portuguese immigrants and their descendants have been neither less nor more ready to accept new cultural patterns than any other group. Few of the first-generation Americans (i.e., native-born children of immigrants)[10] know the language of their parents well, if indeed they know it at all. The religious patterns have undergone changes quite comparable to those, say, of Italian immigrants. American food, furniture, dress, appliances are all eagerly sought. American films, music, recreational activities, and social behavior are generally preferred over the Portuguese. The aura of traditionalism—accepted even by the Portuguese-Americans as part of their identity—is spurious but is one of the devices which shores up the total profile and insures the continuance of boundaries between Portuguese and non-Portuguese. Further it has had the effect to some extent, of a self-fulfilling prophecy, particularly in the area of educational goals.

What of the theoretical significance of the material? Primarily, one must stress the multiplicity of identities which may exist for any given group. Not only must one be careful to delineate the origin of any given identity but one must also consider the implications of two or more profiles. What for example is the result of two profiles, insiders' and outsiders', which are incongruent? If congruent which has precedence historically? How realistic is the identity which insiders believe outsiders hold of them? What effect does cultural identity have on the individual personality and on decision formation?

Another question is posed by Barth's (1969:21) argument that fluidity in the patterns of recruitment or ascription creates a variety of processes which effect changes in individual and group identity. There is no question that there has been variability in ascription and probably recruitment as well, assuming the normal processes of cultural change in the islands; and certainly the processes of change which recruitment and ascription variability set into motion have occurred. Yet the changes in group identity which should have been brought about by these processual forces do not seem to have occurred. We have the interesting situation of an identity persisting in time despite the fact that most models of change would argue for its alteration—particularly when that identity had little basis in fact but was the usual superficial and ethnocentrically biased view of a subordinate group by its economic overlords.

The data argue for the acceptance of both a mythical identity and an analytical identity, the one being that which is stated to be the profile and the other a statement of behavioral reality.

Finally one must explore the implications of identity profiles and the boundaries which are created by them. What are the restrictions and links which those on either side of the boundary see as operating? To what extent does identity determine the type and intensity of network formation between groups in a plural society? What effect does this, in turn, have on action-group formation? What in fact is the relationship between social networks in a complex society and identity formation, stabilization, and change?

Most importantly I have stressed the need to look at the historical raison d'être which underlies all cultural identities. Without an understanding and as thorough a grasp as possible of the context of contacts, one cannot understand sociocultural forces which operate to create any identity.

NOTES

1. Support for the fieldwork upon which this study is based was granted by the Research Foundation of the State University of New York (1972). My thanks to my colleagues in the field: William Leap, Frances White, Maria Lydia Spinelli, and numerous informants, all of whom contributed generously to the study. I alone am responsible for the content of this paper.

2. Plus the Portuguese of Toronto and London.

3. The outsiders' characterization is often categorized as an ethnic stereotype and is exemplified by the so-called music hall or joke book characters (cf., Pat and Mike, Mrs. Nusbaum, "dumb Polack—or Swede" jokes, etc.). The insiders' and the investigator's views may be considered as emic and etic statements. Although there are many common aspects of the identity profile, the position of the Portuguese in California, Hawaii, and other areas of the world differs considerably from that of the New England settlers.

4. See Barth's (1969:23) discussion on the identity-switch of the Sudanese Fur.

5. The communities were Rochester and Corning, New York; Provincetown and Fall River, Massachusetts; Newark, New Jersey; Toronto, Canada; and London, England.

6. Figures given by Bannick (1917:39-41) dramatize this lack. A selection shows the differences. Of immigrants over the age of fourteen who could neither read nor write, the following figures are given for the years 1899-1910 "by race or people": African, 19 percent; Armenian, 23.9 percent; Chinese, 7 percent; Croatian and Slavonian, 36.1 percent; Cuban, 6.3 percent; East Indian, 47.2 percent; North Italian, 11.5 percent; South Italian, 53.9 percent; Japanese, 24.6 percent; Lithuanian, 48.9 percent; Mexican, 57.2 percent; Pacific Islander, 24.7 percent; Portuguese, 68.2 percent; Scandinavian, .4 percent; Spanish, 14.5 percent; Syrian, 53.3 percent; Turkish, 59.5 percent. A study by Keerock Rook and Associates (1972:27) for the Fall River City Planning Board states that, "58.8 percent of persons 25 years of age and over in the state have completed

high school . . . 25.6 percent in the City of Fall River [have done so]." It should be pointed out that those with a better education might not immigrate from Portugal, or would leave the economically depressed area of Fall River.

7. New England maritime interests led to the adoption of the phrase *captain of industry* with the obvious historical leap from ship captain to industrial leader.

8. I define the Sambo stance as behavior adopted by a subordinate group which it perceives to be congruent with the identity imputed to it by a superordinate group. It is agreeable behavior and is often characterized by a large percentage of child-like or simple traits. Such a stance makes a group "invisible" and is a comfort for the "superior" group (since they are not challenged by reality) and a defense for the "inferior" group. It creates a sense of noblesse oblige on the part of the dominant group or at least an attitude of affability which enables the subordinate individual to achieve some advantage in given transactions.

9. In Newark the Portuguese young people have recently taken to sporting T-shirts emblazoned with the words *Portuguese Power*. Though largely treated as a joke, some people were upset by the attention which it attracted to the Portuguese. Still others failed to understand the joke—or the threat.

10. There is disagreement between sociologists and anthropologists on this point. Anthropologists follow common usage while sociologists refer to immigrants as first-generation Americans and the first generation of native-born offspring as the second generation of Americans.

REFERENCES

Bannick, Christian John, 1917. *Portuguese Immigration to the United States: Its Distribution and Status* (A.B. thesis, Stanford University, 1916). (Reprinted 1971, San Francisco: R. and E. Research Associates.)

Barth, Fredrik, ed., 1969. *Ethnic Groups and Boundaries—the Social Organization of Culture Difference* (London, George Allen and Unwin).

Keerock Rook and Associates, 1972. *The Final Report of the Fall River Community Renewal Program* (Alexander, Maine: Keerock Rook and Associates).

Klewin, Thomas W., 1973. Western Island Whaling Grounds. *Yankee* January 1973:68-75.

Taft, Donald R., 1923. *Two Portuguese Communities in New England* (Ph.D. diss., Columbia University). (Reprinted 1969, New York: Arno Press and *The New York Times*.)

Urban and Rural Identities in East Africa: A False Dichotomy

Gary P. Ferraro

Universal definitions of cities have been suggested by social scientists from a variety of perspectives.[1] Any definition of an urban area implies the definition of a nonurban area, for the characteristics of the one are the logical opposites of the other. Redfield (1941) makes explicit this inherent comparison with his folk-urban or rural-urban typology. The implications common to all of these statements, however, are unmistakable; town and country are distinct communities, and discrete urban and rural identities are observable phenomena in the empirical world.

Social science literature abounds with studies regarding socio-cultural patterns in urban areas. The overwhelming majority of these studies fall into two fundamental types: the gross, deductive, polar typologies, which contribute little to our understanding of rural and urban identities for they deviate from reality in the sense that, as Weberian ideal types, they lack precise empirical referents; and the more recent empirical studies that concentrate exclusively on the urban end of the dichotomy and simply impute differences for the rural end. Campbell and Stanley (1963:6) refer to this type of research design as the "one shot case study" in which "a carefully studied single instance is implicitly compared with other events casually observed or remembered." To be told for example that a certain percent of adult urban respondents visit their parents at least once per week tells us very little about rural-urban differences, nor indeed do they tell us whether such differences exist at all. Here again no opportunities for verifying distinct rural and urban identities exist because, with very few exceptions, such studies lack control groups by which to assess the meanings of these ofttimes carefully calculated urban patterns. This fundamental flaw in research design limits the use of the great bulk of recent urban literature for determining the nature of rural and urban identities in various parts of the world. To examine rural and urban identities which discrete socio-cultural systems imply, we must design empirical investigations that account for both rural and urban populations at the same point in time and utilize comparable data-gathering strategies.

In response to this need this paper seeks to determine the applicability of a rural-urban identity model to the Kikuyu of East Africa. The data were collected from 174 Kikuyu residents of the Riruta section of Nairobi and 124 Kikuyu from Lusigeti sublocation in rural Kiambu, Kenya.[2] The relative proximity of traditional Kikuyuland to Nairobi has allowed for the identification of two distinct types of Kikuyu urban residents: nonmigrant, property-owning Kikuyu who have lived in Riruta most of their lives and whose land has been incorporated into the city and Kikuyu from more distant parts of Kikuyuland who have resided in Riruta for less than five years and who approximate our commonsense definition of migrants. These two categories within the Riruta sample I have called respectively "Old Time Residents" and "New Arrivals."[3]

Extensive participant observation, biographical interviewing, and formal questionnaires were the three primary data-gathering techniques utilized to determine whether separate patterns of social interaction differentiate rural from urban Kikuyu, or if we can speak legitimately of an urban, distinct from a rural or traditional Kikuyu cultural identity. An underlying premise assumes that we can infer identities from social and cultural patterns of behavior. That is, if rural and urban populations consistently demonstrate differences both in their patterns of social interaction and in their values and attitudes, then we can reasonably infer that they identify with one or the other of these life styles.

Our data do not even remotely suggest the emergence of a distinctly urban set of sociocultural patterns or the existence of even an incipient separate urban cultural identity. To be certain, changes have occurred in traditional Kikuyu institutions. Many of the traditional institutions and the attitudes and values associated with them no longer exist. Many of the younger Kikuyu informants from both Lusigeti and Riruta, for example, could not relate to me even the purpose of the *guciaruo ringi* (second birth) ceremony, much less any of its details. On the other hand, some traditional practices such as bridewealth, male circumcision, and those associated with naming children have been largely retained. The central point, however, is that there appears to be no marked difference between urban and rural residents on many measures of modernity.

We gathered large quantities of data on the adherence to traditional institutions by the rural and urban samples. Selecting from that material we will examine briefly the extent to which our rural and urban samples conformed to the values and attitudes associated with three such traditional practices—the second birth ceremony, naming practices, and polygyny.

The Second Birth Ceremony. Traditionally an important Kikuyu rite of passage, second only to circumcision, is the rite of symbolic rebirth. Practiced widely by all Kikuyu clans, children of both sexes were expected to experience this ceremony. Although the age of the children varied considerably with the ability of the father to provide the required sacrificial goat, the rite generally involved only children under the age of twelve. The ceremony itself reenacted the birth of the child replete with cries of labor pains, symbolic cutting of the cord, and washing the child after "birth." If the child's father was dead, another elder, usually related, provided the goat. Similarly if the mother was dead, a surrogate mother substituted, although such a woman "is looked upon in the future by the boy as his own mother" (Routledge and Routledge 1910:152). Until the male child was born again, he could not, according to Kikuyu tradition, assist with the disposal of the body of his deceased father, be initiated, inherit property, or take part in ritual.

Turning to the data from Lusigeti and Riruta concerning the rebirth ceremony, considerably fewer numbers of urban males had undergone the rebirth ceremony compared to rural males. The difference, however, reflects the relatively large proportion of younger men in the urban population. Moreover owing to the lack of choice on the part of the person being reborn, a better indicator of the retention of this tradition may be the desire by respondents to have their children participate in the rebirth ceremony. The rural and urban samples revealed substantially no differences in the frequency either of those who have given their children this ceremony or who intend to do so in the future.

Traditional Naming Practices. Immediately upon birth the Kikuyu child is named according to the traditional custom. The first male child receives the name of his paternal grandfather and the first female child receives the name of her paternal grandmother. The second child of each sex receives the name of the maternal grandparent according to sex. It is thought that the child perpetuates the existence of the grandparent after whom he or she is named. This equation in naming between ego and his or her second ascending generation reflects their relatively informal and equal relationship.[4]

Again no significant differences emerged in the extent to which the rural and urban samples continue to practice the traditional pattern of naming children. To illustrate, among the first-born male children of respondents, 5.0 percent of the rural Lusigeti sample, compared to 2.5 percent and 7.5 percent for the New Arrivals and Old Timers respectively, were not named after their paternal grandfathers. Furthermore there was very little variation among the three samples in deviations from the customary practice of naming the first-born daughter after the paternal grandmother. Thus, whereas the traditional *guciaruo ringi* rite has diminished in importance in both rural and urban areas, the customary Kikuyu naming practices have been tenaciously retained in both.

Polygyny. Polygyny in traditional Kikuyu society is the ideal type of marriage. Customary law holds that "a man may have as many wives as he can support, and that the larger one's family the better it is for him and the tribe" (Kenyatta 1962:167). The high value placed on polygyny relates, at least in part, to the fear that a man's family group will terminate if he has no sons. The extinction of a kin group has far reaching implications for the Kikuyu system of ancestor worship.[5] Should all living members of the group die out, the ancestor spirits lose contact with the earth because there is no one with whom to communicate. Furthermore polygyny plays an important structural role in the overall integration of the acephalous Kikuyu society. Since the *mbari* (lineage) is the exogamous group, each wife that a man takes creates a set of strong affinal links between his *mbari* and the *mbari* of his bride, thereby creating a mutuality of interests and responsibilities between the two lineages. A popular Kikuyu proverb reflects the strength of these affinal bonds: *"Kaimba ka muthoni na muthoni iguaga hamwe"* ("In-laws are buried together," the implication being that affines will die if necessary for a common cause).

Examining the practice of polygyny as a measure of the extent to which rural and urban Kikuyu adhere to traditional institutions, the Lusigeti residents, both men and women, reported the highest incidence. Although polygyny appears to be more widely practiced in Lusigeti than in Riruta, the difference was more a function of age than of urban residence. That is when controlled for the age variable, these differences disappear.

We collected data on other measures of traditionalism as well—for example the adherence to such practices as circumcision, marriage payments, and consultation with medicine men. The data indicate the same absence of differences among rural Kikuyu and the two categories of urban Kikuyu. Differences between rural and urban areas in both the practice of and attitudes toward these three traditional institutions were insufficiently large or consistent to indicate any general trends. In short, little in these data suggest that rural Kikuyu residents are decidedly traditional, that urban Kikuyu are decidedly modern, or that urban residence necessarily leads to a noticeable degeneration of traditional ideas and practices.

Sociocultural theories distinguishing between town and country usually assume that the city functions as a melting pot capable of reducing the many ethnic elements to a common cultural denominator. In response to the political necessity to develop a national identity, there has been a general trend in postindependence Kenya to minimize the importance of tribalism. The late Tom Mboya (1969:101) for example has stated that "our urban centers are . . . an important means of bringing together people of different tribes, thus promoting understanding of each other." However, traditional values, institutions, and patterns of behavior persist in East African cities. Although, to varying degrees, urban areas throughout the world have served both to bring people together as well as to break down their cultural distinctiveness, East African cities—and Nairobi in particular—appear to be more salad bowl than melting pot.

A central proposition of the rural-urban identity model posits as one of the consequences of urbanization the substitution of secondary group relationships for primary group relationships. When applied to man's most typical primary group, the family, the rural-urban identity construct sees a progressive, unidirectional isolation and nuclearization of family ties when confronted with modernization and urbanization. Although this notion has been restated in one form or another for centuries,[6] recent discussions of the alleged effects of the city on family relations originate with Wirth (1938:20) who speaks of the "weakening bonds of kinship, and the declining social significance of the family."

Our data from East Africa suggest no such atrophy of kinship relations among the urban Kikuyu. Of the many aspects of kinship behavior on which we gathered data, formal associations of kinsmen—i.e., those involving structured meetings of lineages or sublineages—represent a particularly revealing expression of family solidarity among rural and urban Kikuyu. Prior to European contact Kikuyu society was organized according to nine mythically validated clans and their constituent lineages (*mbari*). It is impossible to derive from existing ethnographic accounts the frequency of formal *mbari* meetings during precolonial times. The central place of the *mbari* within the general fabric of traditional Kikuyu society, however, is well documented. It is probably safe to suggest, therefore, that the *mbari* functions less as a corporate entity today than in former times. However, this overall reduction of the corporate nature of Kikuyu lineages—in large part a consequence of the change in the land tenure system—is not a function of urbanization or urban residence. In fact our data indicate that corporate *mbari* activity is greater among the Riruta Old Timers than among the rural Lusigeti residents. Approximately twenty-three percent of the male Old Timers periodically attended meetings of the *mbari*, compared to only twelve percent of the Lusigeti males. Among the male New Arrivals twenty percent regularly attended such meetings, and in all cases these meetings were held in their rural homestead areas. Furthermore the frequency of *mbari* meetings among the male Old Timers was greater than among the Lusigeti males. Most Old Timers convened on a monthly basis compared to only two or three times a year for the rural men. Many of the New Arrivals, who averaged approximately four to five *mbari* meetings per year, expressed a desire to attend more frequently but were prohibited by the high cost of transportation home.

Prior to the Mau Mau Emergency, that area which is today Riruta had belonged to two lineages, *Mbari ya Marigu* and *Mbari ya Gatharimu* (also known as *Mbari ya Kinyanjui*). Whereas traditionally *mbari* meetings were held to discuss matters relating to marriage payments, land, and war, today they are largely economic in nature. That is, the overwhelming majority of those attending regularly scheduled *mbari* meetings described the meetings as primarily concerned with collecting funds for purposes of investment. One such *mbari* for example has formed a cooperative society with 144 active members. This lineage-based cooperative meets monthly and is administered by a twelve-member executive committee. Officers are elected, minutes of all meetings recorded, modern techniques of accounting employed, and the services of a licensed solicitor have been obtained. Significantly, the oldest living member of the *mbari*, who is in his eighties and is the acknowledged head of the *mbari*, is not a member of the executive committee because it is felt that he is out of touch with modern principles of investment economics.

Instead he and three other elders of the lineage have been elevated to advisory positions without any voting power in matters of investment.

Rural-based corporate lineages are also very much alive, and extend beyond narrow geographic boundaries. The case of Samuel Ngugi, a twenty-five year old New Arrival from Ndeiya Location illustrates their vitality. Samuel, a housepainter earning a salary of 450 Kenya shillings ($64.00) per month, makes the twenty-four mile trip to his home several times a year expressly to attend the formal business sessions of his *mbari*. Even though Samuel is a relatively young man, he has a large stake in the *mbari* cooperative, having contributed more than a thousand shillings. During the month just prior to the interview with Samuel, his *mbari* had assumed the title deed to a 1,851-acre farm in the Ndeiya area for which they had paid 200,000/- KS (approximately $28,000).

These data indicate that it is misleading to think of urban lineages and rural lineages as discrete entities. Rather, because of the ever-increasing opportunities for spacial mobility in contemporary Kenya, lineages that have an urban base, such as those of the present-day Riruta Old Timers, include active lineage members living in rural areas as well as in urban areas other than Nairobi. And conversely, many of the active members of rural-based lineages may reside in urban areas. The structural and functional changes in lineages that have occurred since precolonial times have created a very fluid situation which defies classification according to the sole criterion of rural or urban residence. From fairly localized groups of kinsmen involved with a wide range of social activities and basing their decisions on particularistic considerations, lineages have become non-localized groups of kinsmen concentrating on a more specialized set of activities (primarily economic) and basing their decisions on universalistic principles.

Although the urban residents from our sample attended formal lineage meetings in greater numbers and with greater frequency than the Lusigeti residents, the relative access to capital between Riruta and Lusigeti and other rural Kikuyu areas may explain the difference. The disparity in cash income between Lusigeti and Riruta is considerable (50/- KS per month as compared to 377/- KS per month respectively). After purchasing the basic necessities in Lusigeti, very little remains to invest in a cooperative venture. And since the formal aspects of lineages throughout Kikuyuland involve primarily, if not exclusively, economic cooperation, formal *mbari* activity would of course be greatest in those areas which represent the most affluent Kikuyu.

The proposition that urbanization brings with it the demise of primary groups in general and the nuclearization and isolation of the family in particular implies the concomitant rise in secondary group relationships among urban dwellers.[7] One of the most striking findings of the present investigation has been the general lack of Kikuyu participation in secondary economic and recreational organizations located in Nairobi. For example the Kikuyu have no formal association comparable to the Luo Union. This is no doubt at least partially a function of traditional Kikuyuland's relative proximity to Nairobi. Because of the proximity many Kikuyu residents of Nairobi can maintain networks with kin and friends from home, diminishing the need for urban voluntary associations. Of special interest is the large percent of New Arrivals who actively participate in rural-based organizations. The most commonly found types of Kikuyu rural-based voluntary associations are economic cooperatives formed among *rika* members (age mates) or former rural neighbors. To illustrate, more than ninety percent of all male New Arrivals actively contributing to economic cooperatives belonged to cooperatives that were based in their rural home areas. Such membership entailed both attendance at meetings as well as financial contributions. The participation in rural-based voluntary associations among the Riruta New Arrivals was greater than in any other type of secondary group associations, including labor unions.

The nature of these rural-based economic and social cooperatives which draw part of their membership from urban residents can perhaps best be illustrated by examining a specific case. The Ndeiya Women's Poultry Keepers Cooperative Society Ltd.,[8] consisting of a twelve-woman executive board and approximately 250 shareholders, is atypical only to the extent that its members are all women. The majority of Kikuyu cooperatives tend to be male although cooperatives consisting of both sexes are not uncommon. Since 1949, members have contributed cash (in some cases from the sale of eggs and chickens) which has been recorded and systematically deposited into a Nairobi bank by a member's husband who serves as a salaried bookkeeper/accountant. Although theoretically no limitations on membership exist, there are in fact no non-Kikuyu members. Members do not receive dividends, but rather all interest and profits from their investments are plowed back into the general fund. As an indication of this particular cooperative's assets, within the period of the present investigator's field research the cooperative invested approximately 56,000/- KS (roughly $8,000) in a Fiat bus which runs between Limuru and Nairobi and was considering the purchase of a second bus. The executive board meets regularly every Saturday afternoon to accommodate the members who live and work in Nairobi. Although the majority of the members are rural residents, there are an appreciable number of Nairobi residents, both general shareholders and executive board members, whose urban connections have been very helpful in making investments, in obtaining legal advice, and in bringing pressure to bear, for example, on the Transport Licensing Board from whom a license was obtained to operate their bus.

Conversely, a considerable number of rural Kikuyu residents actively participate in and contribute money to Riruta-based voluntary associations. The central point that cannot be overemphasized here is that the voluntary associations to which contemporary Kikuyu belong (like the corporate lineages) are not closed rural or urban systems, but are rather very fluid organizations in terms of recruitment of membership and cannot be characterized as serving exclusively or even predominantly rural or urban residents.

To understand why the classical rural-urban identity model does not apply in Kenya, we should examine the nationwide economic structure, a structure described by one economist as a "dual economy" (Seidman 1970:13). This duality, a legacy of the colonial period, is comprised of an "export enclave" on the one hand and the "rural hinterland" on the other. The export enclave, represented in Kenya by Nairobi and to a lesser degree Mombasa, is characterized by large, oligopolistic firms from developed countries abroad, employing modern means of production and relatively cheap labor, who are engaged in the production and exportation of certain natural resources as well as in the importation of certain high-priced finished goods. The rural hinterland, characterized by traditional agrarian subsistence economics with the most elementary technologies, supplies the export enclave with cheap, unskilled labor.

Seidman's use of the terms *export enclave* and *rural hinterland*, however, is misleading in that it implies another rural-urban dichotomy. Rather than the spacial or geographic aspects of the dual economy, the significant dimension relates to occupational and economic mobility. The export enclave includes a very small percentage of the total population of Kenya and is comprised primarily of European and American expatriate executives and a token number of African elite. They hold the top paying positions, retain virtually all of the decision-making prerogatives, and are in a position to increase substantially their already superior wealth through judicious investments, hard work, and good fortune. In short they hold the most prestigious and best paying jobs within the private sector of the economy and possess the greatest opportunities for economic advancement.

The other segment of the dual economy is made up of the vast majority of Kikuyu and other Africans from all parts of the country. Some hold school certificates (i.e., are high school graduates); the more fortunate of these are employed as clerks, salesmen, office assistants, theater ushers, waiters, tour guides, drivers, etc. for salaries usually not exceeding 500/- KS per month (approximately $70.00), and usually considerably less. Those with less education hold even lower paying jobs or are unemployed. Although it is difficult to draw a precise line separating the two segments of the dual economy, the critical division is not between rural and urban, but rather between the "haves" (those having both high paying jobs and economic mobility) and the "have-nots" (the unemployed, underemployed, and those whose wages are low and whose potential for upward financial mobility is near zero). And with only several unusual exceptions all people in both the rural and urban samples of this study qualify for the so-called rural hinterland segment of Kenya's dual economy.

Because of the manpower surplus in Kenya and its resulting cheap labor, the export enclave is able to realize considerable profits which eventually make their way back to Europe and America. A major consequence of this drain of capital, of course, is to maintain the separation of the two economic spheres. The important point here is that most (i.e., all but the elite) Kikuyu, irrespective of place of residence, do not have a real share in the corporate profits of the export enclave. They participate in the export enclave only as wage employees, and even this role tends to be insecure. Occupational mobility for most Kikuyu within this private sector of the Kenya economy is minimal.

Rather than thinking of the flow of manpower as a unidirectional recruitment of labor from rural hinterland to the export enclave, it may be depicted more accurately as a circulation of labor from the rural hinterland to Nairobi and back again. Both urban employment and residence in Nairobi manifest considerably high turnover. In western countries laborers tend to relocate more permanently in cities with their families, expecting to stay longer than several months or perhaps a year. In many parts of Kikuyuland—and throughout East

Africa—the men, generally, are the migrants and sooner or later return to their families in the rural areas. This very ephemeral nature of the East African labor force—so characteristic of the Kikuyu—was recognized as early as 1939 by Benson (1939:35) and has led more recent observers to use such terms as *perpetual newcomer* and *returnee* (McElrath 1968).

Within the nationwide economic structure in Kenya, the urban and rural sectors are not isolated or discrete populations but rather are closely interrelated. Given the economic superstructure within which the New Arrivals must operate, the retention of ties to the rural homeland and the unwillingness to commit oneself fully to an urban way of life appear to be the most rational choices the migrant can make. The majority of unskilled laborers as well as the numerous persons holding school certificates have little job security in the face of sickness, accident, or old age. A man suddenly left jobless always has recourse to his rural *shamba* (farm) or that of his kinsmen. Moreover by keeping his wife and children on a rural farm, the Kikuyu migrant actually maximizes his income, for the rural land can usually support his family and in some cases can actually add income through the sale of cash crops. Given the high cost of supporting a family in urban areas such as Nairobi, only the small Kikuyu elite can afford that luxury. Irrespective of freehold plots created by the program of land consolidation,[9] much land is still controlled by lineages or segments of lineages, and inheritance of land to a large degree still takes place within the elementary or the polygynous family. If the migrant opts to sever all connections with his rural homeland, he is in effect relinquishing his rights to the inheritance of his father's land, which in the case of most urban migrants, remains his one and only retreat from the insecurities of urban employment.

The Kikuyu migrant to Nairobi in no way wishes either to identify himself with or to make any social or economic commitment to the city, due in large part to a widely held antiurban set of attitudes. On numerous occasions for example informants expressed their dissatisfaction with the divided city of Nairobi. Those parts of the city in which most nonelite Kikuyu can afford to live are associated with high rates of crime, overcrowded and unhealthy conditions, and unreasonably high rents, while the more attractive residential areas are the domain of the small African elite as well as the Europeans and Asians who have stayed on since the colonial period. Moreover when New Arrival male respondents were asked where they considered their homes to be, only one mentioned Riruta. The remaining forty-three respondents opted for either that rural area in which they were raised and in which most informants have a claim to land or some other rural area where they have acquired land.

All these strands of evidence characterize the rural and urban sectors of Kenya not as isolated or discrete populations possessing analytically distinct sociocultural patterns and identities but as part of the same social system. In light of the national dual economic structure—which impels Kikuyu urban residents to maintain strong economic and social ties with their kinsmen wherever they may reside—a rural-urban identity typology will remain inappropriate for the Kikuyu or other peoples in Kenya until a significant transformation of the economy occurs to break the cycle of the dual economy by permitting greater social and occupational mobility for Africans and by freeing working class urban residents from exclusive dependence for their security upon kinsmen. Until such a change occurs in Kenya's economic structure, the rural-urban identity model is as unexportable to this area of East Africa as are political ideologies.

NOTES

1. For example, an archeological definition has been set forth by Childe (1950); demographic definitions by Jefferson (1931), Willcox (1926), and Duncan (1951); and sociological definitions by Redfield (1941), Sjoberg (1955), Weber (1958), and Wirth (1938).

2. The research on which this paper is based was carried out between September 1969 and September 1970 and was sponsored by the National Institute of Mental Health (grant number ITO1-MH12045-01).

3. Four basic criteria were employed in distinguishing between these two categories. First, New Arrivals have been residents of Riruta for less than five years. Since this served as the primary criterion, there were no exceptions. Second, New Arrivals rent rather than own houses. There were two exceptions in the sample of seventy-two, but both of these were women who had married Old Timers. Third, New Arrivals do not consider Riruta to be their home. There was one exception here. And finally New Arrivals do not own or cultivate plots in Riruta. There were four exceptions here, three of whom were cultivating temporarily until they had saved sufficient capital to invest in low cost housing for rental purposes.

4. A woman, for example, will call her grandson "my husband" and her granddaughter "my co-wife" while a man will refer to his grandson as "my equal" and his granddaughter as "my bride" (Kenyatta 1962:17).

5. Traditional Kikuyu religious beliefs are based on sacrifices to both ancestral spirits and a High God (Ngai).

6. This argument with varying degrees of emphasis on the family dimension has appeared in such distinctions as "status-contract" (Maine 1864), "Gemeinschaft-Gesellschaft" (Toennies 1957), "societas-civitas" (Morgan 1964), "mechanical-organic solidarity" (Durkheim 1933), "primary-secondary" (Cooley 1909), "folk-urban (Redfield 1941), "folk-state" (Odum 1953), "communal-

associational" (MacIver and Page 1955), "familistic-contractual" (Sorokin 1947), and "sacred-secular" (Becker 1950).

7. This notion was forcefully put by Wirth: "Being reduced to a stage of virtual impotence as an individual, the urbanite is bound to exert himself by joining with others of similar interest into organized groups to obtain his ends. This results in the enormous multiplication of voluntary organizations directed toward as great a variety of objectives as there are human needs and interests" (1938:22).

8. In order to preserve the anonymity of the cooperative members, a pseudonym has been used.

9. The Land Consolidation Program was a post Mau Mau Emergency scheme designed to reorganize land holdings into larger units so as to make them better suited for cash cropping. Even though the scheme did consolidate small holdings into larger ones and granted title deeds, the anticipated revolution in Kikuyu land tenure did not occur for several reasons. First, the new holdings, although larger than the average holdings under the former system, were not sufficiently large to allow profitable cash cropping. And second, even among those title holders who had "economic units," sufficient capital was not available to permit cash cropping. As a result most of the new title holders were pressured to absorb more and more of their landless and unemployed kinsmen onto their consolidated holdings. Thus the larger, supposedly economic, land units have reverted to their former state of having to support relatively large numbers of subsistence-farming kinsmen.

REFERENCES

Becker, Howard, 1950. Sacred and Secular Societies. *Social Forces* 28:361-375.

Benson, W., 1939. Some International Features of African Labour Problems. *International Labour Review* 39:35-45.

Campbell, D. T., and J. C. Stanley, 1963. *Experimental and Quasi-Experimental Designs for Research* (Chicago: Rand McNally).

Childe, V. G., 1950. The Urban Revolution. *The Town Planning Review* 21:3-17.

Cooley, Charles, 1909. *Social Organization* (New York: Scribner).

Duncan, O. D., 1951. Community Size and the Rural-Urban Continuum. In *Cities and Society*, P. K. Hatt and A. J. Reiss, eds. (Glencoe: The Free Press), pp. 35-45.

Durkheim, E., 1933. *The Division of Labor in Society* (Glencoe: The Free Press).

Jefferson, M., 1931. Distribution of the World's City Folks. *Geographic Review* 21:446-465.

Kenyatta, Jomo, 1962. *Facing Mount Kenya* (New York: Vintage Books).

MacIver, Robert, and C. H. Page, 1955. *Society* (London: Macmillan).

Maine, Henry, 1864. *Ancient Law* (New York: Scribner).

Mboya, T., 1969. The Impact of Modern Institutions on the East African. In *Tradition and Transition in East Africa*, P. H. Gulliver, ed. (Berkeley: University of California Press), pp. 89-103.

McElrath, D., 1968. Introductory: The New Urbanization. In *The New Urbanization*, Scott Greer, et al. eds. (New York: St. Martins Press), pp. 3-12.

Morgan, Henry L., 1964. *Ancient Society* (Cambridge, Mass.: Harvard University Press).

Odum, Howard, 1953. Folk Sociology as a Subject Field for the Historical Study of Total Human Society and the Empirical Study of Group Behavior. *Social Forces* 31:193-223.

Redfield, Robert, 1941. *The Folk Culture of Yukatan* (Chicago: Chicago University Press).

Routledge, W. S., and K. Routledge, 1910. *With a Prehistoric People* (London: Edward Arnold).

Seidman, Ann, 1970. Comparative Development Strategies in East Africa. *East Africa Journal* 7(4):13-18.

Sjoberg, G., 1955. The Pre-Industrial City. *American Journal of Sociology* 60:438-445.

Sorokin, P. A., 1947. *Society, Culture and Personality* (New York: Harper and Brothers).

Toennies, F., 1957. *Community and Society* (East Lansing: Michigan State University Press).

Weber, Max, 1958. *The City* (New York: The Free Press).

Willcox, W. F., 1926. A Definition of "City" in Terms of Density. In *The Urban Community*, E. W. Burgess, ed. (Chicago: Chicago University Press).

Wirth, Louis, 1938. Urbanism as a Way of Life. *American Journal of Sociology* 44:1-24.

A Stratification of Labyrinths: The Acquisition and Retention of Cultural Identity in Modern Culture

ARDEN R. KING

IT has long been a tenet in social science that individuals and societies acquire an identity through socialization and enculturation. This reciprocal phenomenon has been variously termed. Because man's environment is culture and is the means whereby he becomes human, cultural identity seems the most appropriate term to use. Through a distinctive mode of learned behavior the individual is provided with the means for acquiring a concept of self, and the continuity of the society is ensured. Thus cultural identity is the self-identification made by the creators and inheritors of a given culture history. More completely cultural identity might be defined as the human means of achieving an existential identity that is global in terms of experiential definition and total in the sense of awareness.[1]

All of the traditional ways of explaining how cultural identity is acquired are well known and rationally logical. For anthropologists whose experience and data have been drawn mainly from small societies with relatively homogeneous cultures, there has been the unstated assumption that individuals in a society will acquire a sufficient sharing of attitudes, values, and associated behaviors so that an identity sufficient as a socially unifying mechanism will result. Sociologists, social psychologists, and social historians mostly have used models of small town and rural society to apply the concept of cultural identity to complex cultures and their histories, and they have been affected by much the same limitations as anthropologists. We are struck by the fact of cultural identity but fail to delineate the nature of the phenomenon and how it can operate in all sorts of cultures and individuals with sufficient uniformity to be transferable from one individual to another and from one generation to another. How does cultural identity persist? How is it retained from one period to another in the face of content and even structural changes in the culture?

Can the concept of cultural identity as used by anthropologists be applied in all cultural situations? The structural, let alone the content differences between cultures are striking. Further, is the retention of what appears to be cultural identity in the wide range of historical cultures the same phenomenon? If so, how is it retained in individuals operating in the increasingly discrete behavioral worlds of civilizations? Present anthropological models may not apply to the acquisition and retention of cultural identity in complex cultures. As cultures have become more complex, the necessity has arisen for consciously held, unifying concepts in order for cultural identity to exist. Such phenomena as standardized language, the national state, organized religion come into play, and we question if we are dealing with the same phenomenon in all cultural configurations.

We wonder if cultural identity in the ethnographic and historical sense is a fading and weakening concept. Have such ideas been derived from the investigation of small societies with relatively restricted cultural alternatives for behavior and from the historical abstractions that the contemplation of long sweeps of time affords? Or both? If such is the case, the idea of cultural identity in civilizations is a wishful imposition of the romantic ideal of natural man on civilizations by historians and anthropologists. Do the differences in culture—tribal, peasant, civilizational—provide different modes whereby individual personalities acquire cultural identity? And can we conclude that while cultural identity may remain phenomenologically the same, the mode of acquisition and retention is vastly different when we compare tribal and peasant cultures with civilization?

There have been important structural as well as content changes through cultural history, and it may be that cultural identity is more easily attained in simpler cultures with their smaller cultural content and their restricted structuring of experience and knowledge. Although the mode of acquisition of cultural identity is assumed to be different, we may be dealing with the same phenomenon.

What characterizes the individual in modern culture? Contrasted with the relatively unsegmented culture of tribal and peasant life, a civilization presents a bewildering array of behavioral patterns. However, just as we find that peasants have been incorporated within civilizations despite their relatively restricted world, so too do we find civilization restricting the world of possibility for its members.

For while many behavioral patterns are available to the total society, only a restricted number are available to any one individual. Early cultures provided entire life modes for individuals by ascribing nearly total behavioral patterns to statuses within the total society. Thus particular marriage rules, economic activity, religious behavior, etc., evoked one another. In tribal and village situations almost a complete rank order coincidence exists among the roles an individual plays in all the status systems he occupies.

In civilization through the nineteenth century an analogous condition obtains, and the class systems of western Europe represent a relatively late expression of this phenomenon. A person occupying a particular rank in the religious system could be assigned with a high degree of certainty to a comparable rank in almost any other status system thus verifying the reality of classes. Even so fragmentarily described, we can see that with reference to status consistency the sociocultural environments in which individuals acquire cultural identity did not greatly change from the days of tribal mankind through most of the history of civilization. Is modern culture a different breed of cat altogether?

One of Lévi-Strauss's most evocative metaphors is that of the *bricoleur*. The evocation is that of the developing human presented with the necessity of using organizing principles to deal with the infinity of possible experiences. Like a *bricoleur*, he faces the task on his own in a do-it-yourself fashion, adapting his set of conceptual tools to the particular experiences that confront him. He selects and arranges his percepts and concepts, including some and excluding some. In the process he sufficiently shares experiences and modes of structuring with others so that the unique experiences that result in a unique individual insure both self-identity and social solidarity. The *bricoleur* still lives, but in the circumstance of modern culture he becomes *le bricoleur intensifié*. The individual is more self-consciously a *bricoleur*, and we can rightly ask whether such a phenomenon as cultural identity exists for him—at least in a form comparable to that in other cultural circumstances.

Modern culture confronts the developing personality with a wholly different prospect than in the past. Learning one aspect of the culture does not easily predispose behavior in other aspects. The metaphor of the mazeway (Wallace 1961:16-20) (and those concepts which preceded it) is less and less applicable. A mazeway implies a specific route to given goals, and by learning these one learns the culture. The idea of the labyrinth seems a better metaphor.

Here the individual is not bound by a stricture to discover the pre-ordained structuring of experience through a specific mazeway. Instead he is inserted into an aspect of culture, the content of which he begins to organize, constrained only by the boundaries of permissible behavior. The individual constructs a route representing his own organization of the content to a core of the cultural stratum. But before he completes the construction of the first labyrinth he finds himself translated to another cultural stratum where the process begins again. In a lifetime one will construct many labyrinths and undergo many translations from one stratum to another. The relative independence of these cultural strata provokes a closer consideration of the routes between them. For the developing personality these routes increasingly provide the means of reconciling the differing ranks he occupies in the status systems of each stratum and thereby also the means of achieving an integrated personality. We further suggest that these routes constitute the means of gaining cultural identity in modern culture.

The foregoing contends that the acquisition and retention of cultural identity today may be entirely different from those processes in the past. The rapidly decreasing number of societies with cultural identities of long duration support the contention. We have the quasi-cultural identities of Irishness, the Pan-Celtic movement of western Europe, and the romantic Pan-Indianism of the Americas, but these are not what we have defined as cultural identity. It is, therefore, of interest to examine societies which have retained cultural identity in the face of extended and intense interaction with more complex cultures. Perhaps this will tell us something about the identity processes in modern culture. Let us turn to two examples, the Alta Verapaz in northern Guatemala and the Alte Land in Lower Saxony, northern Germany.

The Alta Verapaz has been analyzed in detail in other publications (King 1972, 1973). From approximately the ninth century A.D. this area has retained a high level of distinctiveness. The influence of pre-Columbian Mexican domination in the post-Classic did not destroy the cultural identity so evident in archaeological and oral history. The domination by the Spaniards was not achieved through conquest but by the reservation of the area as a whole, the Verapaz, under the tutelage of the Dominicans. For nearly three centuries, ca. 1540 to 1820, there was comparatively little Spanish influence and dominance of the sort so typical of the remainder of Middle America. Even after independence the area did not immediately open itself to the ingress of Ladinos, although the Baja Verapaz more rapidly came under the control of Ladinos, thus differentiating the Alta and Baja Verapaz culturally and politically. By the time the Ladinos had begun to settle in this heavily populated, Indian area, the commercial possibilities of coffee planting as well as of several other agricultural products became evident. Because these ventures needed capitalization, northwestern Europeans began to settle the area before Ladino domination could be established. This was especially true of the Germans. They brought the mechanism by which the Alta Verapaz was incorporated into the modern world, i.e., the commercial exploitation of coffee. Through a series of complicated interactions—economic, marital, familial, religious, educational—the Germans and other western Europeans incorporated themselves into the culture. Most significant in this process was the acquisition of a distinctive cultural identity so that they, like the Kekchi Indians before them, became people of the Alta Verapaz. In the middle third of the twentieth century the increase in Ladino population was not accompanied by a national or an ethnic identity, but instead they also adopted a cultural identity that was the Alta Verapaz. A series of complicated status systems developed whereby the individual devised his own coordination of self- and cultural identification. In exemplification of the process proposed above, a proportion of the population, especially those in the towns, put together their own unique combinations of roles and rankings in the existent status systems. Despite structural and content changes of the culture and periods of domination by foreign cultures, the cultural identity of the Alta Verapaz has been maintained. In a less intense way than our second area, the Alte Land of northern Germany, the Alta Verapaz demonstrates the proposals we have made about the individual in modern culture.

The Alte Land[2] is one of those lowland marsh-like areas situated on the lower Elbe River between its mouth and Hamburg. The Alte Land extends down river on the west bank from the old course of the South Elbe to the Schwinge River. Such areas are distinguished from the higher dry lands known collectively as the Geest. The differences in culture between the two play an important part in our conclusions with regard to cultural identity.

The Saxons are known to have settled on the west bank of the Elbe by 200 A.D. In the course of the ensuing nine centuries they diked and drained land. However, there were few Saxon settlements in the Alte Land. The other low-lying areas towards the mouth of the Elbe and the Geest came under full Saxon control.

In the twelfth century new but ethnically and linguistically related peoples appeared in the area between the lower Weser and lower Elbe. These were the Dutch or the Hollanders who had previously contracted with the archbishop of Bremen to drain and settle lowlands between the Ems and the Weser. By 1140 they were applying their knowledge of reclamation to all the areas between the lower Weser and lower Elbe. The area most affected by the Dutch settlers was that with the smallest number of Saxon occupants: the Alte Land. The ensuing reclamation laid down settlement patterns which are still visible today. Dutch settlement can be recognized by the systematic division of the land into regular, narrow strips from the banks of the Elbe inland. Saxon settlement radiated irregularly from the contours of the smaller river courses. In time the Saxon land pattern came to follow the Dutch pattern more and more, although Saxon vestiges are still evident. The first Dutch settlers built houses and began cultivating on the higher lands of the natural levees of the Lühe, Este, and Elbe rivers. They were a varied lot: small farmers, handicraftsmen, shippers, fishermen, store owners, and traders. From the very beginning the variety of culture contrasted with the nearly uniform, full peasant orientation of the Geest and the low areas down river from the Alte Land.

One can write a history and a psychocultural characterization of the Alte Land based upon the building and maintenance of dikes and drainage systems and the effects of the great floods of the Elbe. Indeed one can argue that the fear of, the preparation for, and the battle against the great floods constitute an old and persistent force in an always culturally varied society.

The twelfth to fourteenth centuries saw the rivers confined to their present courses by dikes. The Alte Land had also come to be divided into three distinct areas, the three Meilen. These divisions of the Alte Land, formed by rivers cutting across it and entering the Elbe, persist to the present day.

Although great cooperation and planning between the settlers themselves and between them and whatever political authorities were concerned were obviously necessary, it was the constant threat of destruction by the great floods that gave impulsion to unity and cooperation. In the fourteenth and fifteenth centuries great floods created wastelands, and large areas of the Alte Land were abandoned. But by the end of the fifteenth century most all of the Alte Land had been rediked. In the process interlocking dike and drainage associations came into being. These were mostly affiliated with the individual Meilen. However, on occasion there was unified action by all three leading to an accommodation between Saxon and Dutch law systems although certain differences always remained.

The political independence of the Alte Land in large part immediately derived from these circumstances. A decline in independence was associated with the changes in the law systems connected with the dikes and drainage systems. Briefly the history of the dike law and its application can be divided into two main phases. During the first phase the marshy areas early developed their set of laws—complicated and unwritten—out of practice and use. This applies to all the low regions of northern Germany. The second phase of the dike law coincides with the development of noble and royal power when the dike law was codified and made uniform beginning in the middle of the sixteenth century.

From the fifteenth century on, drainage, protection, and maintenance of the land against the floods and for the increase of productivity were challenged by disasters of monumental proportions—and advanced by engineering feats to match. Interaction with Hamburg increased, even though the Alte Land remained under the political tutelage of Bremen and later Hannover. The main markets of the Alte Land and the chief sources of aid and financing for flood control were in Hamburg.

The first settlers, mainly Dutch, were not fully devoted to year-round agricultural activity. Herein lay one of the contrasts between them and the Saxon peasants living on the Geest and in the downriver marshlands. The settlers practiced generalized farming and animal husbandry to begin with; but by the middle of the fourteenth century specialized fruit raising, especially of apples, became the main economic activity of the Alte Land. The traditional peasants and the fruit growers followed different yearly cycles. A fulltime, traditional peasant was tied to a year-long cycle of activity all concerned with production. The fruit specialist was only seasonally involved in the production of his crops. The specialization enhanced the variety of life in the Alte Land. Specialized produce demands trading activity, and much of the year was spent in marketing. The first markets were the neighboring towns of which Hamburg was the largest. Water transportation, the easiest route to markets, conduced not only to trading but to fishing and shipbuilding. In the centuries to come there would also develop the tradition of seafaring and in the late eighteenth and the nineteenth centuries, commercial shipbuilding. There were always many more varied roles for the Altlander to play than was the case for the traditional peasant.

By the sixteenth century a major struggle had arisen between the archbishops of Bremen and the city council of Hamburg for power and influence over the Alte Land. The former had a just claim to political suzerainty, the latter to economic suzerainty. The archbishop of Bremen placed a ban on Hamburg beer, and Hamburg banned Alte Land fruit. The "Beer or the Cherry War" was waged between 1581 and 1641. By the end of the mutual bans more than a century of wars as well as major storms and floods with consequent severe water saturation of the land had curtailed production. In the late eighteenth century when production returned, the Altländer built ships and sailed to trade in northern Germany and neighboring countries. In the last half of the nineteenth century international trade of fruit became a major undertaking. The English demand for fruit to make marmalades, jams, and liquors was extremely heavy. Internal German trade developed as well. Competition from North American fruit growers came by the end of the century, and two developments arose in answer. First it became apparent that better varieties of fruit were needed and that more scientific modes of production must accompany them. Second land holdings began to be consolidated into larger units. The growing romanticization and idealization of the noble, all-around peasant began to militate politically against the specialized fruit growers. But the Altländer were already a group set apart. By the late sixteenth century they had been noted for their sharp trading activities in the eyes of the city dwellers. This opinion holds to the present day. As one present-day Hamburgian says, "The Altländer are pirates who call themselves peasants."

One last and very important aspect of the economic life needs to be mentioned. Because most of this land was "new," it had never been effectively under the control of political authorities. Many families and properties go back to the fourteenth century, if not before. Most properties have been freehold since the sixteenth century. This contrasts directly with the neighboring peoples of the Geest who have not been free for much more than a century. A history of relative political autonomy combined with the rise of the dike societies and associations and the varied economic activities entered into the distinctive development of the Alte Land.

The new land, the dike and drainage associations, the nearly independent jury systems, plus the relative weakness of noble and royal overlords created political independence. What suzerainty there was amounted to a very complicated interlacing of customary law, church law through parish rights, the fluctuations of the fortunes of small German states, and the ever-increasing influence of Hamburg. With the rise of political entities imposing formal legal codes, the loss of political independence began. This process is first apparent in the Swedish and Hanoverian influence in the seventeenth century. Once begun the process intensified and nearly all autonomy was lost by 1850. This loss was signaled by the elimination of the patrimonial law systems whereby the Dutch descendants had maintained a special position for centuries. The dike and drainage associations were deprived of all but advisory and honorary roles in 1937. What the Swedes began Hitler ended.

Although the archbishop of Bremen had initiated the settlement of the Alte Land, the direct influence of the church never seems to have been very great. The monastaries of the Premonstratensians and the Benedictines controlled some land and received some tithing, but their influence was lessened by the fact that most was new land given in the freehold. The most important role of organized religion devolved upon the parish churches which became the social and legal centers.

The outside world has been a continuous presence in the Alte Land. But the outside world has been of a varied nature. There has always been the opposed world of the Geest and the complete peasant. Fishing as a seasonal activity offered alternatives to the fruit grower or his sons. The rise of fishing as a major activity for Altlander families in the North Sea during the nineteenth century and in the oceans of the world during the twentieth expanded their cultural experience. The nineteenth and especially twentieth century development of shipbuilding served as an entrance into the industrial world.

Finally the influence and dominating presence of Hamburg continuously increased. A brief reading of history shows a strong dependence on Hamburg for relief from flood disasters and for financing the reconstruction of dikes and drainage systems. Hamburg was always the most accessible source of funding. The dike associations more than once played Hamburg against Bremen or Hannover for these purposes. Possibly more important was the Alte Land's nearly complete dependence on Hamburg as a Hanseatic city-state for trade. By way of Hamburg the world beyond the Elbe was always at hand.

The late twentieth century sees the Alte Land experiencing an increasing involvement with the outside world and some serious physical encroachment on its own edges. Its continued specialization in fruit production seems assured, but only with genetic engineering of new varieties of fruit, scientific cultivation and storage, and the rise of highly efficient marketing cooperatives. With the pollution of the Elbe, fishing has declined. Fishing vessels must now go to the North Sea and beyond. Family producers no longer control trading activities although some are still influential in the cooperatives. The encroachment of modern industry is visible. Directly upriver in Hamburg-Harburg, major oil, chemical, and other manufacturing plants run twenty-four hours a day. A gigantic ship-building industry operates in the same area. Downriver, the Dow Chemical Company and an atomic reactor of the North German Electric Commission survey the low plain of cherry and apple trees. Deep into the Alte Land foreign workers recruited to work in these industries have settled in camps on land rented by fruitgrowers.

These are not the only invaders. The Alte Land has for more than a century been a favorite outing spot for Hamburgians. A bucolic stroll through the marshlands filled with fruit trees and the salubrious and expansive view from the Elbe dike draw great numbers on good days. Suburbia encroaches more and more as the Alte Land becomes feasible as a permanent residence. But many of the suburbanites are Altländer or their descendants returning from the city.

But with all this, Altländer and their descendants—both in the home territory and in adjacent areas—retain strong cultural identity. Their history prepared them for the retention of this identity. The many and varied roles available to the inhabitant through time, and the many social interactions with the outside world, have always made these specialized "peasants" capable of entertaining the complexities of behavior attendant on urban life. As Mendras (1970:241) points out in his study of French peasants, horticulture and aboriculture are conducive to a true urbanization of the countryside. The Alte Land may be one of those rare cases of preparation for the modern world that has, at the same time, retained a long tradition of cultural identity.

What then is an Altlander? He is first of all independent and highly ethnocentric even though he has extensive knowledge of the modern world and participates in it. He glories in his reputation as a difficult person to deal with. His emotional attachment to all aspects of fruit production is pervasive, particularly during blossoming and harvest, even though he may not presently be engaged in it nor has anyone in the family been since great-grandfather. Especially does he identify with the dikes and the floods that have destroyed them so many times in the past seven centuries. The land was created by his ancestors, and the old family houses are full evidence of this identity. He maintains cultural identity through religious participation in family weddings and christenings even if he is no longer resident. And he more likely marries an Altlander than not. Perhaps as insightful as anything else of his strong cultural identity as an Altlander is his reputation for refusing to accept refugees from East Germany, either during the war or now.

Alta Verapaz and the Alte Land as examples of the acquisition and retention of cultural identity provide us with some insights into the same processes in modern culture. To a certain extent the peoples of Alta Verapaz and the Alte Land long ago began their acquaintance with the stratification of labyrinths. The very ability to accommodate seemingly disparate roles successfully may mark the distinctiveness of modern man. The Altländer certainly learned to do this. Perhaps the locus of cultural identity in modern culture lies in the shared experience structured by the routes of translation from one labyrinth to another. This does not mean that the routes utilized are identical for all individuals. Their importance rests upon their availability as the means of coordinating an individual's roles (labyrinths). Without them an integrated personality would be impossible in modern culture. This timid assertion smacks of mystical structuralism, but it is no less explanatory than are the concepts of nation state, national language, or the universal church in hypotheses concerning cultural identity in modern civilization.

NOTES

1. "Existential identity" can be conceived of as one that an individual experiences at any given moment and in any given circumstance. To be "global in experiential definition" implies totally encompassing all experience, past and present, so that a definition of existence can be attained. To be "total in the sense of awareness" infers the adumbration of any possible experience for an organism.

2. The most important historical sources consulted are Klenck and Scheidt 1929, Köhler and Riediger 1970, Mangels 1957, and Siemens 1948.

REFERENCES

King, Arden R., 1972. The Impact of Urban Culture on Northern Guatemala. *Verhandlungen des XXXVIII. Internationalen Amerikanistenkongresses*, Band 4:299-302 (Munich: Klaus Renner Verlag).

———— 1973. Coban, Alta Verapaz: History and Culture Process in Northern

Guatemala. *Publications of the Middle American Research Institute,* No. 37 (New Orleans).

Klenck, Wilhelm, and Walter Scheidt, 1929. *Niedersächsische Bauern 1: Geestbauern im Elbe-Weser-Mundungsgebiet* (Jena: Gustav Fischer Verlag).

Köhler, Bernd, and Hans Riediger, 1970. *Das Alte Land* (Reinbek bei Hamburg: Perten Druck Verlag).

Mangels, Ingeborg, 1957. *Die Verfassung der Marschen am linken Ufer der Elbe im Mittelalter: eine vergleichende Untersuchung ihrer Entstehung und Entwicklung* (Stade: Selbstverlag des Stader Geschichts- und Heimatvereins).

Mendras, Henri, 1970. *The Vanishing Peasant: Innovation and Change in French Agriculture* (Cambridge: MIT Press).

Siemens, H. P., 1948. *Der Obstbau an der Niederelbe.* Veröffentlichungen des niedersächsischen Amts für Landesplanung und Statistik, Reihe A. I., Band 27 (Hannover).

Wallace, Anthony F. C., 1961. *Culture and Personality* (New York: Random House).

Discussion

John E. Williams

Let me first express the real delight I found in these papers, all of which reflect a willingness by the authors to deal head on with the fascinating complexities of human behavior. Perhaps my reaction is due in part to the stuffiness of my own discipline of psychology, which sometimes seems to put the rigor of the method ahead of the significance of the inquiry. In any event, I found the papers to be refreshing and stimulating reading.

Before proceeding to my comments on the individual papers let me say a word about my approach to this task. I assumed that in inviting me to react to the papers you wanted me to respond as a person whose training and work is in the field of psychology. In composing these comments I have tried to remain faithful to this assumption and to share my reactions with you in an open and unedited fashion. I realize that by letting it all hang out I run the risk of being naive just at the point where I think I am being profound, but if so, let it be.

I found Richard Robbins's paper ("Identity and the Interpersonal Theory of Disease") to be a worthy contribution to the emerging view that illnesses of all sorts should be viewed as disruptions in living. Dr. Robbins's proposal that a person's health is a function of the degree of consistency between his self-, public, and social identity is reminiscent of Carl Rogers's emphasis upon the importance of congruence in one's perceptions of self, ideal self, and others in the maintenance of psychological health (Rogers and Dymond, 1954).

For a long time physicians and psychologists have tried to ignore the evidence that some very ill persons can be restored to health through nonscientific procedures such as the ceremonies conducted by witch doctors. Physicians and psychologists have also tried to conceive of illness as consisting of processes internal to the individual and have minimized the fact that all human beings live in a network of social relationships. When an individual becomes ill, the usual pattern of social relationships is upset—the individual is disturbed, and so is the primary group.

The increasing evidence of the importance of psychosocial factors in so-called physical disease is forcing a broader view of medical problems; the pursuit of the germ is no longer the one clear path toward good health; the isolation and sanitization of the patient may be doing as much harm as good. The fact that the isolation and sanitization of modern hospital treatment can alleviate certain aspects of certain types of illness should not make us content to settle for this. Let's have our cake and eat it too! We can appreciate progress in medical science while still maintaining pressure for a proper recognition of the psychological and social aspects of illness. We can insist that hospital visiting hours and facilities be arranged to meet the needs of the patient and his family and not the convenience of the hospital staff. We can ask that fathers and even siblings be allowed to participate in the act of childbirth. We can follow Tom Szasz (1961), admit that mental illness is a myth, and learn to talk instead about problems in living. We can quit talking about disturbed children and recognize what Virginia Satir (1969) and others have been saying all along; namely, that it is the relationships in the whole family which are disturbed, and that it is the whole family which needs to be treated.

Dr. Dobkin de Rios ("Cultural Persona in Drug-Induced Altered States of Consciousness") provides a valuable documentation of the effects of hallucinogenic drugs in situations where drug use is a normal and integral part of a culture. For example her findings show that Peruvian Amazonians under the influence of ceremonial drugs tend to experience what their culture has told them they should expect to experience. Put this way we see a certain parallel between these hallucinations and the mental states induced by suggestion and hypnosis. What a person thinks about and how he feels about things are heavily influenced by his culture; if the culture instructs him in an expected reaction to ceremonial drugs, then his reaction tends to conform to cultural expectation. The drug bends the mind, but the new shape is still culturally patterned.

This view helps provide an explanation for the idiosyncratic and often bizarre responses of Westerners to hallucinogenic drugs. In this case drug use is not ordinarily an integral part of the socialization process—to the contrary Western culture takes a negative view of altered states of consciousness. With this background the use of drugs by the Westerner is usually a nonconformist rather than a conformist act. Having no culturally defined expectations as to the nature of the hallucinations, the Western drug user's response remains at an idiosyncratic level—when the mind bends, it bends in personally rather than culturally patterned ways.

Dr. Dobkin de Rios provides us with a perspective concerning the often encountered notion that the use of hallucinogenic drugs leads to a new level of experience which may have mystical and religious significance. This seems clearly to be the case in the traditional groups which Dr. Dobkin de Rios describes. On the other hand, we also see that the mystical and religious components of the experience are contributed not by the drug per se but by the expectations which the user brings to the experience, which in turn are the outgrowth of the socialization process.

Dr. Orso ("Folklore and Identity") underscores a need for a balanced approach to the study of folklore—a balance between an interest in panhuman identity, and ethnic identity. It seems rather trite to have to remind ourselves that all human groups are the same and also different. If we study products of group behavior such as folklore, we will find evidence of both the similarities and differences among human groups. I understand that all human societies have some sort of sexual taboos; but of course the details of the taboos differ markedly from group to group. Why has it been more difficult to take such a balanced view with regard to the study of folklore? It may be because the study of folklore has often been undertaken from a particular ideological viewpoint, whether or not this bias was recognized by the researcher. Instead of being studied in a detached and objective fashion, folklore has been too often employed, as Dr. Orso says, to argue that all peoples are the same and therefore equal, or to argue that all peoples are different and have the right to be so. Thus folklore researchers have entered their work with an ideological axe to grind and, not surprisingly, have found just what they needed to hone their blades.

I have another thought. Perhaps the basic nature of folklore invites ideological bias. After all, the content of folklore often deals with the central and majestic themes of human existence and, thus, has the appearance of being intrinsically more important than other social products. If I can use folklore to prove my point, I have appropriated a most impressive weapon. Ideology aside, it remains to be seen whether folklore warrants some special status or whether its unique appeal is largely illusory with other, more mundane social products being equally valuable as raw materials for the understanding of man.

Dr. Manning's ("Entertainment and Black Identity In Bermuda") major thesis rests on a sound and ancient psychological principle: anything which is regularly and successfully associated with powerful emotions tends itself to become affect laden. In the Bermudian clubs which Dr. Manning describes, the symbols of Afro-American and Afro-Caribbean identity are regularly associated with experiences of elegance and sexuality, with the result that the concept of Afro identity is becoming infused with powerful positive emotions. If a contemporary colored Bermudian discovers that it feels better to think of himself as Afro rather than British, Dr. Manning thinks that he knows why.

Elegance and sexuality are not always bracketed together. One can think of other situations where they seem to be mutually exclusive, as in some cultures where the upper classes are expected to be elegant and asexual, while the lower classes are inelegant and sexual. The packaging of elegance and sexuality provides an uncommonly powerful mix which would be expected to alter the affective meaning of any cultural symbols associated with it.

The psychologist in me is tempted to reach for my trusty semantic differential (Osgood, et. al. 1957) and to study the similarity in affective meanings of certain concepts among colored Bermudians. Dr. Manning's hypothesis would certainly predict that the ratings of the word *Afro* would be more similar in affective meaning to the terms *elegance* and *sexuality* than would the term *colored Bermudian* or the term *British*. A series of such studies spaced over a period of time might enable one to chart the progress of further changes in the concept of Afro identity in Bermuda.

Dr. Leap's paper on Indian English ("Ethnics, Emics, and the New Ideology") points up the central role of shared language in the definition and development of cultural identity. If I understand Dr. Leap correctly, he is saying that we may oversimplify when we say that you and I speak the same language because we share a common cultural identity. The other side of this coin is the role that a shared language may play in the development of a cultural identity in the first place—if we talk the same language, we must be brothers.

This latter view is of interest with regard to the Indian rights movement and the possible evolution of Indian English into red English. Certainly no one is more aware than anthropologists of the cultural diversity that historically characterized the Indian peoples of North America; the idea of a single Indian culture is a largely fictitious concept which has developed among non-Indians (perhaps because to them Indians all look alike). With the impact of modern education and communications, there has been the development of a Pan-Indian movement which seeks to minimize traditional cultural differences and to unify all Indians into a single group, identified as the victims of the white man's oppression, and devoted to the elimination of the effects of this oppression. In this connection Indian English may come into play as an ideological tool. If we all speak the same language and this language is distinctive from that of our oppressor, then we must be brothers who are separate from the oppressor. Because of this dynamic, Dr. Leap feels that we may see the evolution of Indian English into red English which serves not only a communication function but, more importantly, serves as a basis for belief in the idea of Pan-Indian cultural identity. Dr. Leap points out the paradox in this situation where Indian English, a mark of cultural oppression, may come to serve as a source of identity and pride, which may then be employed in the movement against cultural oppression.

Dr. Leap alludes to some of the parallels between the evolution of red English among Indian Americans, and black English among Afro-Americans. Black English is being given serious attention by some psychologists who believe that the assessment of intelligence among Afro-Americans can be accomplished more effectively through black English than through standard English. An example of this approach is the Black Intelligence Test of Cultural Homogeneity being developed by Dr. Robert Williams at Washington University, St. Louis.

Dr. Parades's "The Emergence of Contemporary Eastern Creek Indian Identity" provides a historical account of the gradual evolution of a sense of Indian identity in a group of Alabama Creek Indians whose ancestors had escaped the Indian Removal of the 1830s and remained east of the Mississippi. I confess that I have some trouble with the historical method. The reading of a detailed account of something which has happened in a certain way does not always give me the sense of scientific progress which it appears to give others. I have the same trouble with the case study technique in psychology. After reading a detailed account of the problems in some individual clinical case, I find myself asking—"How has the presentation of this case advanced our understanding of disturbed persons?" Sometimes the answer is a positive one; sometimes one must admit that one has merely been entertained and not enlightened. I found Dr. Parades's paper to be fascinating reading, and I was particularly impressed by his demonstration of the influence of fortuitous circumstances on the development of Indian identity in this group.

Dr. Smith ("Portuguese Enclaves: The Invisible Minority") points up some of the difficulties in applying an overly general theory regarding the assimilation of immigrant groups into mainstream American culture. There seems to be a basic assumption that once an immigrant group has established a base in this country, the members of the group will then seek to maximize their success and status in terms of the values of the larger community. If in a given situation the group does not behave in this fashion, it is presumed either that the group remains committed to certain old culture values which interfere with the adoption of new values or that the assimilation of the group is being prevented by social forces exterior to the group. Dr. Smith's analysis indicates that neither of these conditions is sufficient to explain the failure of the Portuguese-Americans to adopt the success and status values of the larger community. Perhaps, as Dr. Smith suggests, the key factor here is the "commuter mentality" of the Portuguese groups—historically the Portuguese-Americans shuttled back and forth between New England and the Azores. After all, success and status are always relative terms, defined in terms of certain reference groups. The New England Portuguese have always been well off in comparison with their brothers in the Azores—and perhaps this was the critical reference group. The man who leaves Appalachia to work in the Detroit automobile factory may consider himself quite successful with reference to the folks at home, particularly if he continues to entertain the possibility of returning there himself. The Chinese immigrants who came to build the western railroads provide another instance of high status relative to a home reference group in combination with low status in the general American hierarchy.

The data that Dr. Smith has collected to date are not intended to be quantitatively sophisticated or conclusive. I hope she will continue her studies using techniques which can provide more detailed data concerning her hypotheses. For example the semantic differential method could be employed with literate Portuguese-Americans to study more precisely how they view themselves, their fellow Portuguese-Americans, the Azoreans, non-Portuguese reference groups, etc. A comparative study of such concepts might lead to still further insights into the causes of the assimilation failure in this interesting group of New Englanders.

I found myself having the same general response to Dr. Ferraro's paper on the Kikuyu migrants ("Urban and Rural Identities in East Africa: A False Dichotomy") as I had earlier to Dr. Smith's paper on the Portuguese enclaves. In both cases the usual molar theory did not account for the observed data. As Dr. Ferraro points out, a move from rural residence to urban residence is supposed to lead to certain predictable changes: a shift from a traditional to a modern life style, the substitution of secondary group relationships for primary group relationships, etc. Dr. Ferraro's data provide no evidence of the predicted changes among the Kikuyu who have emigrated from traditional Kikuyuland to Nairobi. Dr. Ferraro's explanation for the failure of the classical rural-urban identity model in this instance is that the Nairobi migrant in no way identifies himself with an urban way of life and still considers his home to be in the rural area from which he migrated. The home identification dynamic in this instance parallels the case of Dr. Smith's Portuguese-Americans.

One is tempted to generalize and say that rural or urban location per se has little to do with identity. Identity is, rather, a function of the persons with whom one feels kinship and the place which one thinks of as home. In other words what Dr. Ferraro calls the classical rural-urban identity model seems to carry an important hidden condition which is required to make it work: the urban migrant must come with the expectation of establishing a new home and new personal associations in the city. When this psychological condition is met, the classical theory probably works very well and the predicted changes do occur. On the other hand Dr. Ferraro shows that in the absence of this condition, the mere fact of urban migration has little impact on the identity of the migrant.

Dr. King's paper ("A Stratification of Labyrinths: The Acquisition and Retention of Cultural Identity in Modern Culture") suggested to me a parallel between the maintenance of personal identity and cultural identity under conditions of modern life. To be prepared to live amidst the flux of our modern world, it is very adaptive for an individual to view himself as one who can tolerate and cope with variety and change. This self-view becomes, in effect, an important part of his personal identity. In a similar way whenever past experience in coping with diversity and change are integral parts of a cultural identity—as with the Altländer—then there is built-in protection against dominance by cultural influences external to the group.

In closing let me say a few words about the concepts of social and cultural identity as they have been employed in this symposium. These concepts are undoubtedly powerful tools in the effort to understand human behavior. One must be careful, however, to remember that cultural identity is not a "thing" but a theoretical construct—a convenient fiction which we employ in our efforts to comprehend the subject matter. The construct is our creature and as such must always be kept open to critical scrutiny. Thus it seems to me that the anthropologist's first question regarding some new human group should not be, "What is their cultural identity?" but rather, "Do these people behave in a fashion which warrants the application of a construct of cultural identity?" As Ashley Montagu (1964) has pointed out regarding the concept of race, we must be careful when we use the concept of identity that we do not take as a given that which is to be demonstrated.

REFERENCES

Montagu, A., 1964. The Concept of Race in the Human Species in the Light of Genetics. In *The Concept of Race*, A. Montagu ed. (Glencoe: The Free Press), pp. 1-11.

Osgood, C. E.; G. J. Suci; and P. H. Tannenbaum; 1957. *The Measurement of Meaning* (Urbana: University of Illinois Press).

Rogers, C. R., and R. F. Dymond, eds., 1954. *Psychotherapy and Personality Change* (Chicago: University of Chicago Press).

Satir, V., 1969. *Conjoint Family Therapy* (Palo Alto: Science and Behavior Books).

Szasz, T. S., 1961. *The Myth of Mental Illness* (New York: Dell).

Discussion

GILBERT KUSHNER

WE are, I think, riders on or at least observers of a bandwagon whose name is Social or Cultural or Ethnic Identity. Our symposium is the latest in a recent series on the topic of identity that began in earnest just a few years ago. And we have seen a spate of publications on the topic in recent years.

Whence comes this bandwagon, and who are its builders, riders, and assorted hangers-on? In the context of ethnicity, Aronson (1971:1) suggests that it arises from a "belated recognition that the societies we were studying had lost their autonomy." Latter-day "radical" or "relevant" anthropologists and even those who are not so labelled may feel that in these times of genocide, racism, colonialism, and despair, we must identify and speak of some persistent, if elusive, quality which provides roots and firm ground for otherwise alienated, powerless, and anchorless individuals caught up in the whirlwind of modern existence—which is all of us everywhere—primitive and civilized alike. And there's money in it too, let's not forget that. HEW, for example, has recently come up with a yet-to-be-explicitly-defined funding program for research in "Ethnic Heritage Studies." In addition there is our increasing concern with studying nontribal man; that is, man living in not so closely bounded social units. Here the notion of identity achieves a perhaps special utility. Thus one might conclude that anthropology, like other scholarly traditions, sails with the tide of the moment.

But the issue of cultural or social or ethnic identity is not really a new one at all. From one perspective it is an issue that has been with us for all of our history as a discipline. For what is identity but another referent for the host of questions, dilemmas, and paradoxes with which we are engaged when we speak of culture? If the notion of identity seems especially beset with difficulty, we may derive some comfort from the continued existence of the manifold

and unresolved empirical, operational, definitional, analytical, and explanatory problems attending that most royal and most maligned conceptual tool we possess as a discipline. And are we not in the end,
under whatever heading—culture, identity, social interaction, network
analysis, ethnoscience, etc.—still asking the same elemental questions:
"Who and what am I?" "Who and what are we?" "Who and what
are they?" "Why and how do I and we and they persist and change?"

Identity just might turn out to be among the most difficult yet,
I believe, among the most fruitful of the concepts we have tried to
utilize in our explorations. Its complexity is attested to by the wide
variation in the papers presented here. Its potential promise is demonstrated by its utility in addressing the wide range of issues discussed
in our papers.

Robbins makes good use of a basic approach dealing with identity
from a social interaction perspective to consider similarities and differences between Western and non-Western beliefs about disease and
therapy. Important in his effort are ideas regarding self-, public, and
social identity. In another place, Robbins (1973) uses the same strategy
in the pursuit of another set of questions regarding economic change,
interpersonal relations, and drinking behavior, the latter viewed in
terms of identity-resolving fora. Here he shows that identity, like
certain statuses, must be validated and affirmed in what he, following
Barth (1969), calls fora. And note that in discussing fora, one becomes
involved with such traditional anthropological notions as core values
and cultural foci. Clearly the identity concept in Robbins's work is
a powerful tool with which to address a variety of issues.

Dobkin de Rios, with abundant illustrative detail, shows how cultural identity is manifested at the deepest levels of awareness accessible through drug-induced experience. This indicates that the lessons
of personal identity, as demonstrated in traditional drug-using societies,
are learned so well as to mask the heterogeneity of personality types.
As she points out, the deepest levels of the unconscious are not to be
separated from the cultural nexus. In terms of the early learning
hypothesis (e.g., Bruner 1956a,b), we are led to think of relatively
persistent identities in this context.

Orso's paper presents evidence demonstrating the historical use
of folklore studies to reinforce and promote two levels of cultural
identity, panhuman and ethnic, especially the latter. She notes that
although ethnic folklore studies are needed to discover universal
patterns and motifs, they are frequently pursued for separatist and
other ethnocentric ends. Yet, as we know, oppressed peoples often

require such symbols of identity around which to rally in order to develop a sense of self-worth. As anthropologists we are increasingly urged by such peoples as well as by some of our colleagues to discover these materials and make them public. This expanding concern with our work, even with what in more tranquil times used to be more esoteric areas of anthropology, will no doubt continue apace in the future. So also will our need to make choices between value-free and value-laden research projects—if indeed such choice exists.

Bermudian blacks' entertainment behavior provides a mechanism through which Manning examines the general issues of boundary exclusion and inclusion. He deals with identity symbols derived from music, style of dress, historical heritage, and from considerations of status affectation, attitudes, and mood, i.e., "tone." Note the range of cultural elements that may be utilized as identity symbols. The identity symbols, together with, I assume, a language of identity, function in institutional settings—the clubs. Given a continued actual or symbolic exclusion from white Bermudian society, these may be the makings of a persistent identity system.

A concept of linguistic identity is offered by Leap as one way to produce a sense of uniformity to combat the otherwise seeming fragmentation of a language community by differing speech styles. In addition it serves as another mode in terms of which to locate identity. His consideration of Indian English, when viewed from the perspective of group linguistic identity, clearly demonstrates the reticulate relationship between identity and experience. As he puts it, identity is formed out of the products of group experience and in terms of that experience. Given the formation of identity, then it, of course, conditions that experience. We are quite rightly urged to keep this in mind when we are proffered such notions as the image of limited good or the culture of poverty as explanatory independent variables. In the case of Indian English, the situation is especially poignant, for as Leap notes, it is a product of the very social forces its speakers seek to overcome. But we have seen similar products turned into positive modalities of identity, as in the case of the contemporary soul movement or in Jewish self-deprecating humor. In these instances also, as with Indian English, we indeed need to direct our attention not only to the products but to the exogenous forces which help bring them about.

In ethnohistorical fashion Paredes relates the emergence of contemporary Eastern Creek Indian identity to the larger sociocultural systems in which Eastern Creeks are embedded—an indispensable need in the study of any society, and particularly in studies of segments of complex societies. Judging from the data Paredes presents, however, contemporary Eastern Creek identity may be conditioned not only by events in the larger social systems, but also by an aboriginal identity which functioned, for example, to generate endogamous marriage and to limit between-hamlet social interaction to special occasions. To put this in another way, the issue addressed may not only be the emergence of an identity, but also the various manifestations of an identity in response to differing external pressures over time.

In the Portuguese case discussed by Smith, their behavioral reality is *not* consonant with the identity which they and others accept as true, and therefore she suggests mythical and analytic identities, real and ideal identities, and proposes we might think about the functions of congruent and incongruent identities for boundary maintenance. Like Leap she mentions the self-fulfilling prophecy dimension of identity. In the context of real issues which face us as students of complex societies, Smith raises worthwhile questions linking networks and network formation to identity formation and maintenance.

Goodenough (1963:176-214) discusses social, personal, public, private, and other dimensions of identity which may be relevant here. Similarly, his recent consideration of "Culture, Language, and Society" (1971), in which he carries further his earlier notion of seven different senses of the culture concept, may be useful. What I have in mind is the possibility of developing equally different senses of the identity concept, and thereby sharpening and extending its utility. Fitzgerald, for example, in his introduction to this volume, differentiates between social and cultural identities. Applied to the Maori he uses the distinction to deal with diverse identities held concurrently which enable an individual or a group to cope with bicultural relationships. We are led to think also of such constructs as operating identity, subjective identity, identity pool, and so forth.

In like fashion Wallace and Fogelson (1965), in the context of total identity with reference to the individual, propose negative and positive subsets, the former composed of feared and real identities, the latter of claimed and ideal identities. Spicer (1972) explicitly notes that identity symbols function importantly as sources of motivation and of prophecy, a self-fulfilling prophetic image.

Ferraro attempts to examine rural and urban identities through a study of Kikuyu. He assumes that differences between rural and urban populations with respect to patterns of social interaction, values, and attitudes, signify differences between rural and urban identity. Finding no such initial set of differences, he concludes that there are no identity differences amongst Kikuyu. I think that the rural-urban and other similar dichotomies need not necessarily have any direct content or structural relation to identity models. They may be dealing with quite different subject matters.

W. H. Auden's "The Labyrinth" contains some lines which seem especially appropriate in the light of King's profound contribution:

> Anthropos apteros for days
> Walked whistling round and round the Maze,
> Relying happily upon
> His temperament for getting on.
>
> The hundredth time sighted, though,
> A bush he left an hour ago,
> He halted where four alleys crossed,
> And recognized that he was lost.

King's statements about the nature of cultural identity, which is the wellspring of self-identity, remind us that the idea has long been with us and that its modes of acquisition in relatively homogeneous cultures are generally thought to be well known. On the other hand in complex cultures, our image of cultural identity, its nature, acquisition, and retention, like other anthropological models derived from less complex cultures, may need revision. He wisely asks how cultural identity is retained in the face of content and structural change in culture over time. The close coincidence between the various status systems in premodern culture makes for relatively little differentiation with respect to individual participation (here I have in mind Linton's usage) in contrast to modern cultures. It may be, King continues, that cultural identity is therefore more a conscious phenomenon for modern man. As the individual over time tries (with increasing desperation, I would suggest) to define and to find his own identity, he moves from one uncompleted labyrinth (*not* mazeway) to another, perhaps, as Auden suggests, getting lost in the end. The labyrinth metaphor and the discussion of labyrinth structure in King's paper provide a stimulating and potentially extremely useful model for understanding identity in complex cultures. There are, he proposes, cultural identities in seemingly stable form that have persisted over long time periods. His sketches of two such identities, necessarily brief and incomplete, seem nevertheless amply illustrative of his major contentions regarding the labyrinth. They are also illustrative of Spicer's (1971, 1972) arguments to which I shall return later.

And so we have seen identity used in these papers as a tool with which to examine a wide range of topics, from disease and therapy to Pan-Indianism to folklore to drug-induced experiences. And therein resides one measure of the power of the concept—its applicability to many specific topical problems.

Earlier in my discussion I called attention to work by Goodenough and Wallace and Fogelson that is instructive with regard to identity. Let me now turn to efforts by Spicer and Freed.

Freed (1957) identified two types of societies which he thought successfully perpetuated themselves: the shtetl and Old Order Amish. The former is distinguished by the presence of class-based specialists whose protected roles focus on the maintenance and elaboration of selected features of culture. I don't think Freed would object if I were to call these selected features cultural identity. The Old Order Amish type possesses strong means of social control through which individuals are enjoined (I now reinterpret Freed to say) to develop appropriate identities. Freed emphasizes internal mechanisms of persistence which are operative in the context of larger, more inclusive systems.

Spicer (1971) has recently devoted an article in *Science* to the topic of our symposium. I can scarcely do it justice in the space remaining to me. Persistent cultural systems, one variety of which has been labelled a nation, a people, or an ethnic group, may be investigated, he suggests, using the concept of identity systems and, in particular, collective identity systems. The latter concept refers to the relationship between a people and selected cultural symbols. Thinking in this way reminds us that there are relationships of meaning between people and their cultural products; necessitates the consideration of "the cumulative character of culture and encourages the search for process" (p. 796); and requires the analysis of individual motivation. Where persistent identity systems exist, there are data indicating some sort of "continued conflict between these peoples and the controllers of the surrounding state apparatus," generally over "incorporation and assimilation into the larger whole" (p. 797). An "oppositional process," then, between the larger system and the people is critical "in the formation and development of the persistent identity system" (p. 797).

Spicer goes on to suggest three sets of internal characteristics and maintenance processes of such systems. One is a set of identity symbols which may include land, language, music, dance, heroes, institutions.

In short, crucial for the supremely adaptive nature of the persistent identity system is the readiness with which *any* sociocultural element may be exploited as an identity symbol at any given historical moment. Clearly this point argues against the need for an equally persistent inventory of sociocultural content. A second area of adaptability is common participation in the language of identity, in values, and in political organization. Again the content of these spheres of participation may change over time. The third area is composed of the institutional means by which persistent systems are maintained. Here Spicer proposes that a wide variety of mechanisms may exist; all however emphasize "a high positive valuation of the local community in some form" (p. 799). In almost an end note he suggests that states, having transformed the energy of peoples into state-level integrations, "regularly break down in the absence of mechanisms for maintaining human motivations in the large-scale organizations they generate" (p. 800).

More recently Spicer (1972) emphasizes that what persists is not a way of life or a culture or even a particular set of cultural traits. Instead only bits and pieces may survive in the form of identity symbols, which capture "in concrete and easily encompassed form . . . historical events in which people see and feel and relive their particular common heritage as actors in history" (p. 7).

Focusing on the general issue of persistence and change in terms of identity may, I hope, signal a significant shift in the direction of our scholarly energies. For too many years we have instead asked questions pointed at change in terms of discrete cultural entities. As one consequence of that concern, we now have as part of our heritage a host of trivial studies in several branches of anthropology focusing on the processes of acceptance or rejection of one or another trait under conditions that are rarely generalizable. Turning our attention to the problem of identity persistence obviously demands a systemic view applied in carefully conceived research designs and requires contributions from all branches of our discipline since we are addressing a question that necessitates cross-cultural and cross-temporal data.

We may now view the notion of identity as a route not only to the kinds of specific topical problems mentioned earlier but also as one way to raise questions about cultural evolution; about the formation, maintenance, and disintegration of the state; and about that most human of our qualities, the need to affirm our solidarity with other human beings.

REFERENCES

Aronson, Dan R., 1971. Ethnicity as a Cultural System. (Paper presented at the annual meeting of the American Anthropological Association.)

Barth, Frederik, 1969. Pathan Identity and its Maintenance. In *Ethnic Groups and Boundaries*, F. Barth, ed. (Boston: Little, Brown), pp. 117-134.

Bruner, Edward M., 1956a. Cultural Transmission and Cultural Change. *Southwestern Journal of Anthropology* 12:191-199.

——— 1956b. Primary Group Experience and the Processes of Acculturation. *American Anthropologist* 58:605-623.

Freed, Stanley A., 1957. Suggested Type Societies in Acculturation Studies. *American Anthropologist* 55:55-68.

Goodenough, Ward H., 1963. *Cooperation in Change*. (New York: Russell Sage Foundation).

——— 1971. *Culture, Language, and Society*. McCaleb Module in Anthropology (Reading, Mass.: Addison-Wesley).

Robbins, Richard H., 1973. Alcohol and the Identity Struggle: Some Effects of Economic Change on Interpersonal Relations. *American Anthropologist* 75:99-122.

Spicer, Edward H., 1971. Persistent Cultural Systems. *Science* 174:795-800.

——— 1972. Catalans, Irishmen, and American Indians: The Problem of Enduring Peoples. (Sigma Xi Winter Lecture, University of Arizona.)

Wallace, Anthony F. C., and Raymond D. Fogelson, 1965. The Identity Struggle. In *Intensive Family Therapy, Theoretical and Practical Aspects*, I. Boszormenyi-Nagy and J. L. Framo. eds. (New York: Hoeber Medical Division, Harper & Row), pp. 365-406.

The Contributors

Marlene Dobkin de Rios, an associate professor of anthropology at California State College, Fullerton, is also research anthropologist at Metropolitan State Hospital, Norwalk, California. Her primary interests are hallucinogens and culture, and medical anthropology. She spent a year in the Peruvian Amazon studying folk healing with ayahuasca, a hallucinogenic vine.

Gary Ferraro is assistant professor of anthropology at the University of North Carolina at Charlotte. His major interests are African ethnography, educational anthropology, and the anthropology of complex societies. He has conducted research in East Africa on the effects of urbanization on traditional family structures and has served as a consultant on the impact of highway construction and urban renewal on local populations in the United States.

Thomas K. Fitzgerald is assistant professor of anthropology at the University of North Carolina at Greensboro. His primary interests are nutritional and educational anthropology. His book dealing with the New Zealand Maori university graduate will soon be published.

Arden R. King is professor and head of the Department of Anthropology, Newcomb College, and research associate of the Middle American Research Institute at Tulane University, New Orleans. His primary interests are in Nuclear America, especially Meso-America, and anthropological theory. He has recently done field research in northern Germany.

Gilbert Kushner is associate professor and chairman of the Department of Anthropology at the University of South Florida, Tampa. He also serves as associate dean of the College of Social and Behavioral Sciences. He has done field work in Israel in an administered community of immigrants from India, and in the United States. His primary interests are in complex societies, urban anthropology, and directed sociocultural change.

William L. Leap is assistant professor of anthropology at the American University, Washington, D. C. Trained as an anthropological linguist, he has worked with pueblo communities in the American Southwest and with Portuguese immigrant communities in Massachusetts and London, England. His interest currently focuses on the language needs of pluralistic speech communities and on the commitments developed by segments of these communities in response to those needs.

Frank E. Manning is assistant professor of anthropology at Memorial University of Newfoundland, St. John's. He is interested primarily in symbol systems, religion, and socioeconomic development. He has done field research in Bermuda and in the West Indies, and has served as visiting lecturer at the Centre for Multi-Racial Studies in Barbados.

Ethelyn G. Orso is associate professor of anthropology at Louisiana State University in New Orleans. Her major interests are folk medicine, Middle America, and making documentary films of folkloristic events. She has done field work in Costa Rica, Mexico, and New Orleans.

J. Anthony Paredes is assistant professor of anthropology at the Florida State University, Tallahassee. His previous research includes studies of Ojibwa and rural whites in northern Minnesota and summer fieldwork in Mexico. His major interests are in contemporary Native Americans, problems of sociocultural change, and the individual in culture.

Richard Howard Robbins is associate professor and chairman of the Department of Sociology and Anthropology at the State University of New York, Plattsburgh. His major interests are in the relationship between economic change and interpersonal relations, the study of belief systems, and interaction and identity.

M. Estellie Smith is associate professor of anthropology at the State University of New York, Brockport. Her research interests include the Pueblo Indians of the Southwest, ethnic enclaves such as the

Portuguese, and maritime peoples. She is book review editor for *Urban Anthropology* and *Studies in European Society*. Her theoretical foci are cultural change, social control, and ethnolinguistics.

John E. Williams is professor of psychology and chairman of the Department of Psychology at Wake Forest University, Winston-Salem, North Carolina. His major research interests are in race and color concepts in young children and adults, including cross-cultural studies conducted in collaboration with J. Kenneth Morland.